The Weekend Genealogist

The Weekend Genealogist

timesaving techniques for effective research

Marcia Yannizze Melnyk

BETTERWAY BOOKS
CINCINNATI, OHIO
www.familytreemagazine.com

About the Author

Marcia Yannizze Melnyk is a genealogist, lecturer, instructor, and author of the *Genealogist's Handbook for New England Research, Fourth Edition* and *The Ancestors and Descendants of Annabelle Whitehead and Anthony Pedro*. She has lectured on all aspects of genealogical research, from beginner to advanced levels, for nearly ten years. She is the creator and instructor for the New England Historic Genealogical Society's "Genealogy 101" course and president of the Italian Genealogical Society of America, Inc. Her other interests include restoration, preservation, and documentation of gravestones, as well as American and Italian history.

The Weekend Genealogist. Copyright © 2000 by Marcia Yannizze Melnyk. Manufactured in the United States of America. All rights reserved. No part of this book may be reproduced in any form or by any electronic or mechanical means including information storage and retrieval systems without permission in writing from the publisher, except by a reviewer, who may quote brief passages in a review. Published by Betterway Books, an imprint of F&W Publications, Inc., 1507 Dana Avenue, Cincinnati, Ohio 45207. (800) 289-0963. First edition.

Other fine Betterway Books are available from your local bookstore or on our Web site at www.familytreemagazine.com.

04 03 02 01 00   5 4 3 2 1

Library of Congress Cataloging-in-Publication Data

Melnyk, Marcia Yannizze
   The weekend genealogist / Marcia Yannizze Melnyk.
      p.   cm.
   Includes bibliographical references (p.) and index.
   ISBN 1-55870-546-5 (alk. paper)
      1. Genealogy. 2. United States—Genealogy—Handbooks, manuals, etc. I. Title

CS16.M45   2000
929'.1'.072073—dc21   00-036110
                                                                CIP

Editor: Sharon DeBartolo Carmack, CG
Production editor: Christine Doyle
Interior designer: Sandy Conopeotis Kent
Cover designer: Melissa Riley/ Tin Box Studio
Cover illustrator: Melissa Riley/ Tin Box Studio

I would like to dedicate this book to the following people:

To my friend Sandra Nickerson Frost, who has been my friend, teacher, mentor, traveling companion, and emotional support for the last ten years of my life. She has taught me the meaning of the word "organized."

To my husband of twenty-five years, Jim, and daughters, Diana and Kate, for all of their support, patience, and encouragement, and lots of proofreading.

To my ancestors, for making my life richer through their stories and lives.

Acknowledgments

There are many people to thank for their encouragement and assistance during this project.

My friend and colleague, Sharon DeBartolo Carmack, began this book project by suggesting me as the author to Betterway and completed the project as my editor. She has been my inspiration, sounding board, and biggest supporter throughout the project.

My friends Sandra Nickerson Frost, Jonathan D. Galli, Michael Leclerc, Jane Schwerdtfeger, and Maureen Taylor provided ideas, proofreading, support, and encouragement in spite of their very busy lives.

Last, but certainly not least, is my family. To my husband, Jim, whose constant support has been crucial to the final product; my daughters, Diana and Kate, who never took me too seriously and helped me laugh at my mistakes; and my mother, Shirley, whose excitement in the whole project has been contagious, I extend my heartfelt thanks and admiration.

Icons Used in This Book

 Case Study — Examples of this book's advice at work

 Printed Source — Directories, books, pamphlets and other paper archives

 Citing Sources — How to cite an unusual source

 Reminder — "Don't-Forget" items to keep in mind

\di'fin\ *vb* **Definitions** — Terminology and jargon explained

 Research Tip — Ways to make research more efficient

 For More Info — Where to turn for more in-depth coverage

 See Also — Where in this book to find related information

 Idea Generator — Techniques and prods for further thinking

  Sources — Where to go for information, supplies, etc.

 Important — Information and tips you can't overlook

 Step By Step — Walkthroughs of important procedures

 Internet Source — Where on the web to find what you need

 Supplies — Advice on day-to-day office tools

Library/Archive Source — Repositories that might have the information you need

 Technique — How to conduct research, solve problems, and get answers

 Microfilm Source — Information available on microfilm

 Timesaver — Shaving minutes and hours off the clock

 Money Saver — Getting the most out of research dollars

 Tip — Ways to make research more efficient

Notes — Thoughts, ideas and related insights

Warning — Stop before you make a mistake

Table of Contents At a Glance

Table of Contents

Introduction, *1*

Introduction

Many of you may wonder why a full-time, professional genealogical researcher is writing a book about the timesaving techniques needed by you, the "weekend genealogist." After all, researching is my job, right? Yes. However, I am not only a professional researcher, but also employed as an instructor and lecturer in the field of genealogy. I would have less time to research my own family if I had not learned how to maximize my time. Over the years, I have conducted research while working full-time in nonrelated fields. I have had to create and implement many of the suggestions offered in this book in order to continue my family history research while taking care of the other aspects of my busy life. Several of my jobs have been in the field of bookkeeping or finance and required many of the skills later applied to my genealogical research.

Even today, as a full-time genealogist, I find my time for actual research is still restricted, sometimes even more than before. No matter what your occupation is, you have time constraints to deal with. Whether you are an at-home mother (talk about a full-time job) or a professional working in your field of expertise, you still must find ways to do the things that you enjoy and will enrich your life. Earning a living always seems to get in the way of fun, doesn't it?

Being organized is a wonderful feeling. Thoroughly looking at a project, establishing a plan, and completing it provides a sense of accomplishment. Since there are many demands on your time, using your research time in the most efficient manner is the best way I know to increase the time you have available for other endeavors.

Throughout this book you will find tips and suggestions on how to organize your completed research as well as how to keep it organized. Researching methods that can be implemented using the Internet, mail, and research facilities, on the weekends or whenever you have a spare minute, will also be presented. Once you start using some of these ideas, you will begin to find other ways to maximize your time. Use all of the tools available to you, and don't waste time lamenting about how little of it you have. Make the most of your time and always remember that time is money.

I have always found that if I make time to do things I enjoy, the less desirable obligations seem easier to accomplish. I have a magnet on my refrigerator that says, "If Momma ain't happy, ain't nobody happy!" I hope this book provides you with some inspiration that you can use, not only in your family history research, but in other areas of your life as well. Enjoy the journey as well as the destination.

—Marcia Yannizze Melnyk

ONE

Forms, Forms, and More Forms

Using standard genealogical forms is one way to help organize your information in a concise and understandable format. A librarian or fellow genealogist can see and understand exactly what you have and what you need. By using these forms, you also ensure that future generations of researchers will be able to decipher your work. We all know that many valuable papers are thrown away or destroyed after a person dies simply because the survivors don't know what they are or mean. Many hours of research can be lost in an instant if the resulting paperwork makes no sense to someone looking at it without your guidance. We understand (most of the time) our own notes and documents as no one else will. But through the use of standard forms, there is a better chance that future genealogists will be able to utilize your work. By showing pride in your work and processing it in a manner that says, "this is important," you will be helping to preserve your research for future generations.

Using standard forms or creating new forms to document your data can be done in conjunction with the organization techniques outlined in later chapters. As you organize the papers, this will help you see what you already have and what you still need. The idea is to document on a log sheet the records that you have already filed. At the same time, you can check to be sure that the information has been transcribed onto the pedigree and family group record sheets or to your computer program before filing. There have been occasions when I have been catching up on my filing and realize I have two copies of the same record. This only occurs when I fail to document it on the proper form in the first place. This rarely happens any more as the good habits are slowly overtaking the bad.

Today we are fortunate to have so many forms and books to acquaint us with the many standard forms that are currently available. **An excellent book showing the many types of forms available is** *The Unpuzzling Your Past Workbook* **by Emily Anne Croom.** Croom not only presents forms that you can photocopy

Printed Source

and use, but also shows creative ways they can be used. Just because a form is intended for one purpose doesn't mean you can't adapt it to another. I have used and adapted many of the forms Croom provided. There are as many different forms as there are books on the genealogical market these days, so be selective. Try out several different ones to determine the one that works the best for your needs. Our grandparents or aunts did not have the choices that are available to us. It can be downright confusing at times.

Many companies sell forms that are actually printed on acid-free paper with acid-free ink, which should always be the forms you use for your permanent copies. Photocopies of these forms can be used as worksheets (observing any copyright restrictions), but the photocopy process uses an acid to adhere the toner to the paper. This type of acid is used by printers to etch brass plates. Need I say more? Hopefully, someone will invent a copier in the near future that can be archival-safe. Also, keep in mind that most laser printers use toner (and acid) in the printing process. Ink-jet printers use ink rather than toner, so they may be a better bet for printing forms. Always use acid-free paper in your printer. Check the packages in the office supply stores to see which are labeled as acid-free.

Definitions

Pedigree chart—A genealogical form that outlines a person's ancestry over several generations.

PEDIGREE CHARTS

One of the most important standard forms is the pedigree chart. This chart can have space for four, five, or six generations, depending on the brand. I prefer the chart with four generations since it is less cluttered and has more room for entering information or notes to yourself regarding later research tips. A standard pedigree chart will usually include at least six fields of information for each individual, as follows:

1. Date of birth
2. Place of birth
3. Date of marriage
4. Place of marriage
5. Date of death
6. Place of death

It may also include date and place of baptism or christening, and perhaps a line for the burial place. Whatever the form, be sure it has these six fields of information. I have always found that if the form does not ask for, or provide a space for, the information, you are more likely to forget to enter it. When filling in any form, do you enter data that is not requested? Probably no. So having a space designated for that information reminds you to enter it.

Some pedigree charts leave off the place of marriage, which I find very annoying. I would rather have the place than the date. The time frame for the marriage is a narrow one; the location could be anywhere. By ensuring that the forms have a *minimum* of these six fields, you will have all the pertinent information you need at your fingertips.

Pedigree Chart

Chart no. _____
No. 1 on this chart is the same
as no. _____ on chart no. _____

8 Beriah CARPENTER   cont. ___
B: abt 1745
P: RI
M: 1773
P: RI
D: Apr 1834
P: S. Huntington, Chitt., VT [newspaper]

4 John CARPENTER
B: 24 Apr 1774
P: S. Kingston, Wash., RI
M: 2 Jan 1799
P: Harwich, Rutland, VT (now Mt. Tabor)
D: 3 Sep 1846
P: Huntington Center, Chitt., VT @ 72y

9 Elizabeth "Betsey" BABCOCK   cont. ___
B: 27 Feb 1755
P: S. Kingston, Wash., RI
D:
P:

2 Calvin D. CARPENTER
B: 14 Oct 1814
P: Huntington, Chittenden, VT
M:
P:
D: 1 Jan 1887
P: Huntington, Chittenden, VT

10 Stephen NICHOLS   cont. ___
B:
P:
M:
P:
D: bef 18 Mar 1788
P: will 5 Sep 1787 - prob. 18 Mar 1788

5 Druzilla NICHOLS
B: abt 1783
P: Danby, Rutland, VT
D: 12 Jun 1852
P: Huntington Center, Chittenden, VT

11 Nancy "Anna" STAFFORD   cont. ___
B: 1761
P: RI
D: 10 Jan 1840
P: Danby, Rutland, VT

1 Malona CARPENTER
B: 1840
P: Huntington, Chittenden, VT
M:
P:
D: 31 Dec 1888
P: Starksboro, Addison, VT

Spouse _____

12 Thomas SUMNER   cont. ___
B: 11 May 1734
P: Hebron, Tolland, CT
M: 7 Jun 1761
P: Hebron, Tolland, CT
D: 4 Jan 1820
P: Near Toronto, Canada

6 Henry George SUMNER
B: 13 Jul 1771
P: Thetford, Orange, VT
M: 25 Oct 1798
P: Family Bible Record
D: 31 Jan 1856
P: Bristol, Addison, VT

13 Rebecca DOWNER   cont. ___
B: 4 Feb 1739
P: Sunderland, Franklin, MA
D:
P:

3 Malona SUMNER
B: 9 Apr 1806
P:
D: 11 Feb 1841
P: VT

14 Asahel HALL   cont. ___
B: 7 Sep 1746
P: Kingston, Plymouth, MA
M: 11 Apr 1771
P: Duxbury, Plymouth, MA
D: 24 Feb 1821
P: Bristol, Addison, VT

7 Sarah HALL
B: 29 Apr 1779
P: Family Bible
D: 13 Nov 1855
P: Bristol, Addison, VT

15 Abigail BARNES   cont. ___
B: abt 1747
P:
D: 2 Jun 1834
P: Bristol, Addison, VT

Prepared 14 Aug 2000 by:
Marcia D. Melnyk
10 Genealogy Drive
Anytown, USA

1

Sample Pedigree Chart

Check your computer program to see if it prints the pedigree chart with all six fields. Some do not. Try printing out the same chart in several different formats, such as four, five, and six generations, and then compare the information on each. Does the program have to truncate, or shorten, any of the data fields to make it fit that specific format? Which format is easiest to read? What information has been deleted, if any? Consider all of these facts when deciding which format to print. Only by comparing the different formats offered can you make a sound judgment as to which is best for you.

Another option that you should check for, and most computer genealogy programs will offer, is a place to put the compiler's name and address. This is a feature that many people neglect to use. This ensures that your name and address are printed on every single form you print from that program. Your name and address should be on everything you take out of your house. If you lose or misplace anything, you have a better chance of recovering it if it is clearly labeled.

FAMILY GROUP SHEET

The second form is the family group sheet. This form lists a couple and all of their biological children. As the title suggests, it contains a family group. Adopted children can be added to these forms as long as you document them as adopted. Since many people use the information they find when researching their ancestors for medical purposes, it is important to indicate if a child is not the biological child of either parent. If a husband or wife has been married before and there are children from that union, they should be included on a separate family group sheet. This form has a place for all of the children and includes all six fields of information as well as the children's spouses' name. This information is very important to your research. Knowing all of the children, where they moved to, and their spouses' names is invaluable when researching the parents. Many times the wife's maiden name does not appear on your ancestor's birth, marriage, or death record, but it may appear on one of his/her sibling's records. Town clerks, clergymen, and others keeping records all had varying degrees of record-keeping skills. Some were very meticulous, and others only wrote down the names of the party or parties involved, if they recorded anything at all. By looking at all of the family members and their individual records, you will find valuable information and clues that will assist you in further research.

Example: When I was researching the Barber family from Mount Holly, Rutland County, Vermont, I accumulated many records for my ancestor's siblings. When recording this information on the family group sheet, I noticed that two of my ancestor's siblings married residents of Alstead and Walpole, Cheshire County, New Hampshire. This caused me to take a closer look at those towns. I discovered that many of the families in the town of Mount Holly, Vermont, and the vicinity had connections to the towns of Alstead and Walpole, New Hampshire. This gave me the possible migratory route for many of my Rutland County families, which has paid off over and

Definitions

Family group sheet—A genealogical form depicting a couple and their biological offspring that is used to record births, marriages, deaths, and other pertinent information.

Case Study

Family Group Sheet

6 Aug 2000

Husband	**Thomas CARPENTER**	
Birth	abt 1709	W. Greenwich, Kent, RI ?
Death		
Burial		
Marriage	4 Jul 1737	W. Greenwick/Westerly RI
Father	Oliver CARPENTER (b abt 1675)	
Mother	Sarah O'KILLEY (?)	

Wife	**Elizabeth PAGE**	
Birth		
Chr		
Death		
Burial		
Father	John PAGE	
Mother	Sarah UNKNOWN	

Children

1 M | **Thomas CARPENTER**

Birth	3 Aug 1738	W. Greenwich, Kent, RI ?
Death		
Burial		
Marriage		

2 F | **Mary CARPENTER**

Birth	17 Oct 1740	W. Greenwich, Kent, RI
Death		
Burial		
Spouse	Christopher BULL	

3 M | **Joseph CARPENTER**

Birth	1741	W. Greenwich, Kent, RI
Death		
Burial		
Spouse	Bethiah UNKNOWN	

4 F | **Elizabeth CARPENTER**

Birth	4 Sep 1742	W. Greenwich, Kent, RI
Death		
Burial		
Spouse	Samuel TEFFT	

5 M | **Beriah CARPENTER**

Birth	abt 1745	RI
Death	Apr 1834	S. Huntington, Chitt., VT [newspaper]
Burial		
Spouse	Elizabeth "Betsey" BABCOCK	
Marriage	1773	RI

Prepared 6 Aug 2000 by:	Comments:
Marcia D. Melnyk 10 Genealogy Drive Anytown, USA	

Sample Family Group Sheet

Tip

over again. It also revealed the maiden name of my ancestor's wife, for which I had diligently searched for more than four years. I had never considered looking halfway across northern New England for her name. Those two siblings' records were complete, including the town of origin for the bride, whereas my ancestor's record did not exist at all! **Every time you record new information on a family group sheet, review the previously recorded research to look for clues.**

Maintaining meticulous records for the entire family group will provide you with clues for further research and will help you locate those ancestors who never seemed to stay put! One of my ancestor's brothers was listed in the family Bible as "Obadiah, born 1806, went west, never heard from." Sometimes I have wondered if these vagabonds were looking for something or running from something! Keeping track of relatives that are constantly on the move can be a real challenge.

There are several criteria to look for when choosing a family group sheet to use. One form is two-sided with enough space to record fifteen children as well as additional notes on the back. (Form #A100 family group sheet produced by Everton Publishers, Inc. See chapter three for contact information.) By having a two-sided form, you will carry fewer pieces of paper. Paper, and our ancestors, can get very heavy after a while! **Things you should look for on the form are:**

Important

- a minimum of six fields for vital information for every person on the sheet
- a place to record residences for the primary couple
- a place to record their religious affiliation
- a place to record other spouses for both the husband and wife
- a place for the names of the couple's parents
- a place to list the occupation of the individual
- a place to record military service
- room to record eight or more children
- a place to record your name, address, and phone number on the sheet

One reason this information is so important is that it will continually prod you to look for it when you are researching. Abundant and concise information on the family group sheet will provide you with valuable information about the individuals and make your research more productive.

When using either one of these two forms, the pedigree chart or family group sheet, there are certain guidelines for properly entering the information. Proper, consistent documentation will make for a more readable record. Besides the obvious—writing legibly—**how you record the information is important. The following formats should be used:**

Step By Step

1. **Surnames of individuals should always be written in all capital letters,** such as Joseph ROUNDS. This helps avoid confusion later as families tend to use surnames as given names for the children. Another reason is that some names, such as John George, do not present an obvious surname. If the name is written as "George, John" the comma is there

to indicate that the last name is first. If and when the comma is left out or is not obvious, the name could be recorded incorrectly, making it very difficult to find in an index. Avoid this confusion by using all capitals for the surname. Keep this in mind when a person does not appear in the records or indexes where they should be. Try reversing the name and looking it up again. I have found many records this way because the clerk either left out the comma or the person indexing the name misread the order. This often happens with immigrants because their names are unfamiliar to the clerks, who record them incorrectly.

2. **Record all middle names, when known, and use initials only if you don't know the given middle name.** By listing the middle names of individuals, you may gain a clue to other relatives' names. Some middle names run in certain families and can be the clue you need when re-searching several people with the same name. Sometimes families use the same middle initial for all of the children, making it easier to pick out possible relatives from records. Some people actually use their middle name rather than their given first name. I have found many people randomly using their first, middle, and nicknames over a given period of time. You must know, and record, these names to be sure to look for them when searching records.

3. **Record nicknames whenever possible and indicate them in quotation marks, e.g., Seneca Baker "Joe" ROGERS.** Record keepers are very likely to record the person under the nickname, especially if it is the name most commonly used by the individual. My grandfather, Seneca Baker Rogers, was called Joe Rogers for most of his adult life. Few official records recorded him as Seneca Rogers; most recorded him as Joe or Joseph Rogers. Knowing this has made finding the records a little more work, but has always paid off. Whenever I check an index under Rogers, I always look for all of the possibilities (Seneca, Seneca B., S. Baker., S.B., Joseph, Joe, Joseph B.). By knowing all possible variations and names, you can do a thorough search in any index.

4. **Always record dates in the following format: 10 Apr 1888.** There are several important reasons for this format. If you write the date as Americans commonly do, 4/10/88, another person, especially a Euro-pean, might interpret it to mean the fourth day of the tenth month instead of the tenth day of the fourth month. The year should also be written out entirely. When records are looked at out of context, it may cause confusion as to whether you mean 1888 or 1988. Look at all of the problems the computer industry had because they dropped the century indicator in dates. They should have listened to genealogists; we have always known the drawbacks of not using the complete date. The month should not be indicated as a numeral, but in alpha format. It can be written in all capitals and reduced to three letters. If you choose to record the month in upper and lower case (Jan, Nov, etc.),

be sure to use all four letters for the month of June, since "Jan" and "Jun" could easily be misinterpreted when handwritten. Note that this format eliminates all punctuation within the date. When dealing with handwritten documents, commas and other punctuation can sometimes appear to be an additional number or change the appearance of the number. Many a comma has been misread as a one. The easiest way to make this a habit is to date your checks in this manner. I always write dates in this format on anything I fill in. I don't even think about it any more.

5. **List the locations with the smallest division appearing first.** Most records will include a town name, although some may also include the name of a township, parish, or smaller village within the town. The proper way to list this is, "Byfield Parish, Newbury, Essex Co., MA." This will indicate to the reader that the record appeared in the Byfield Parish records rather than the town of Newbury's records. If the record appeared only in the Newbury town records, you would record it as "Newbury, Essex Co., MA," indicating the record's proper source. Sometimes they are listed in both places, and sometimes in only one location. By being more precise and specifying the exact location of your source, you will have far more accurate records to build on with future research. Also, depending on where the record was *originally* created, one of these two records will be a primary source and one will be the secondary source. If no town is noted in the record—and in some states, records are only kept at the county level—record it as Cattaraugus County, NY. This indicates that the record was found at the county level.

6. **Always include the county name when recording any location.** Since different types of records are maintained at different levels of government, it is imperative to know all of the divisions. Over the centuries, counties have been divided, creating new counties, and the results can be very confusing. By recording the county name as it existed at the time of that particular record, you will have a more accurate record. Just because a town is located in Worcester County, Massachusetts, now, does not mean it was always in Worcester County. Worcester County was created in 1731 from parts of Middlesex and Suffolk counties. Documents recorded in the original county will probably be held in the county courthouse of the original county, not the new one. Another reason to always record the county is to remind yourself which records you might need to look up in what counties. Remember that records are held at different levels of jurisdiction, and all jurisdictions should be searched.

Spending just a few extra minutes properly filling in these forms will ensure that all of the information is understandable to another genealogist or reference librarian.

RESEARCH LOGS

The third form is the research log. **Many researchers neglect to use this important form to record** *everything* **they look at.** Knowing where you have looked, whether you have been successful or not, not only prevents duplication of research but helps you retrace your steps should you have to take another look at the source of your information. When you go into a library, look in the card or computer catalog to see what books it has that pertain to your research goals. Record the call numbers, titles, and authors directly on the research log, not on a scrap of paper. The reason for this is twofold: (1) Once you look at the book and determine it has no information regarding your search, you can log it as "wrong family," "no information," and so on. *Recording both negative and positive results* will save you many hours in the long run. If you look at a book or census and don't find anything, do you want to look at it again a year from now? Will you remember that you have already looked at it before? If you do not record it on the log sheet, then you are bound to look at it again. Keep a log sheet in the binder along with the family group sheets for that surname or family, depending on the amount of research you do on them. You can also keep log sheets for certain research facilities or localities that you visit on a regular basis. (2) The log sheet can be consulted when you cannot remember where you discovered the source or book.

My research log sheet also contains a column to record how many pages as well as the page numbers that I photocopied from each book or source. It is easy to forget what you copied at a later date and any reminder is beneficial. You should be able to retrace your steps by using your research log, and easily duplicate any information you need to. Remember that the goal is to do it right the first time so that you don't have to redo it later.

Example: I use the Vermont statewide index to vital records quite frequently. I keep one logbook (containing many log sheets) for this facility. I may research three or more families in one trip, and they are all logged in the book together. I will then note on the research log sheet for that surname that I looked at Vermont vital records, including the specifics of the years and names covered. Again, this quick two-step process guarantees that I have everything recorded. If you find it more efficient to log this search on the individual surname research logs, go ahead. For your system to work, it must be clear, understandable, and useable for you.

Many times when you look at a book, you will take notes from the text or photocopy some of the pages. When taking notes, I always use notebooks rather than loose paper. My notes often cover more than one sheet of paper, and I found that I did not always remember to title each new loose page of notes. If, or when, the papers were mixed up, it was difficult to determine what the notes referred to. By using my notebook, my pages always remain in the proper order. I use one of the many brands that is bound, three-hole

Warning

Case Study

Money Saver

Important

Warning

punched, and perforated. This keeps the notes together unless you want to separate them. An additional benefit is that if I drop the notebook, the papers don't fly all over the place.

I always buy my notebooks, binders, index cards, dividers, highlighters, and other supplies in late summer or early fall when the back-to-school sales are on. You can stock up on these supplies and save a lot of money in the process. I also find that when I am in an organizing mood, I get frustrated if I do not have the supplies handy and the mood quickly passes. Being able to lay your hands on the supplies you need, when you need them, is part of getting and staying organized. So keep yourself stocked with supplies!

When I purchase notepads and binders, the first thing I do is label all of them with self-sticking address labels. This serves two purposes: One, they will never leave my house without a label, and two, my kids won't take them. No child wants supplies with Mom's name on them. It works like a charm! I also purchase several folders and binders in very bright colors for special projects.

This brings up another point. **Never leave home without *every* notebook and binder labeled with your name, address, and phone number.** Having worked in libraries and research facilities for years, I know how many researchers leave things behind. You only have to take a look at the lost and found box to see how many researchers lose years of hard work. Most staff members will look into the notebook or binder to see if there is an owner's name. If not, unless you remember where you left it, it's gone! I always put the address labels on the covers so I, or someone else, won't accidentally pick up the wrong notebook. Many look alike. By using one of the brightly colored binders as my traveling research binder, I add a little insurance against leaving it behind or having someone else pick it up by mistake. The brighter and more obnoxious the color, the better. I discovered this by laying a dark green binder on the ground in a cemetery. It took me over an hour to find it. Now Day-Glo orange is my color of choice! I also write the research subject on the notebook with black permanent marker. I use the same notebook for certain family lines rather than mixing them all up.

Never take any original documents out of your house! I have seen researchers with tintypes, original marriage certificates, and precious documents tucked into the front pocket of their binder. Remember, if you lose it, you can't replace it! Any item that you don't want to punch to put in a binder can be inserted into an acid-free sheet protector, which are readily available in most office supply stores.

Most family group sheets and pedigree charts provide a space for your name and address. Using a rubber address stamp for this really speeds up the process. Just remember, every form, binder, briefcase, and pencil case should be labeled with your name and address. Don't take a chance with your valuable documentation. Even a research log should bear identification.

CUSTOMIZED FORMS

The next type of form you will use is customized. Whenever I approach a new type of record, I check how the indexes or documents are recorded. Most have some sort of standard format. I then create a form that follows that specific format. For example, the Massachusetts state vital records indexes are all laid out in the same format:

Surname	Given name	Town of Event	Date	Volume #	Page #
Brooks	Jonathan	Walpole	1911	332	104

By creating a log sheet that follows the format of the specific record, I won't miss needed information and I am able to standardize the information, listing all of it quickly and accurately. I add a column on the far right to make notations as to what action I took. I can record notes regarding photocopies made, abstracted, or transcribed, or note that it was the wrong person in this column (see the log sheet below). I now have a log sheet of every record I've looked at. I use one sheet for each surname or project I am working on so they can be filed with the other research log sheets. Some libraries have the indexes, but not the records themselves, so I do all of my indexing at once and then take just the log sheet and a notebook with me when I look up all of the records at once. Since the Massachusetts vital records office charges three dollars per hour to use the research room, I do not want to pay for the time it takes to index what I need. By indexing at another facility that has no time restraints and pressures, I can do a thorough job before I have to punch that time clock!

**A USEFUL FORM
YOU CAN REPRODUCE**

For a full-sized blank copy of the Vital Records Log Sheet, see page 123. You are free to photocopy this form for personal use.

NAME	TOWN	YEAR	VOL	PAGE	CKED

Vital Records Log Sheet
By creating a log sheet that follows the same format of the records or index you are using, you can list all of the information quickly and accurately.

With the many different software programs available today, it is simple to create a form to fit any need or record group. **Forms can be created using drawing programs or software that is specifically designed to create forms.** Stick with the less expensive ones (there's that frugal New England background creeping in again), as they are usually easier to learn and use. My husband had a software program for making forms that was meant for his business applications. I would have to go back to school to learn how to use it! I purchased an inexpensive program and have never needed to upgrade to anything else. I learned how to use it in a matter of minutes, and I am not exactly a computer whiz. It creates forms in portrait or landscape mode

Idea Generator

**A USEFUL FORM
YOU CAN REPRODUCE**

For a full-sized blank copy of the Vital Records Form for Foreign Country Research, see page 124. You are free to photocopy this form for personal use.

(vertical or horizontal format) with as many lines and columns as I want. If I will be making a lot of notes, I make each entry line wider to accommodate this.

Some of these forms have evolved as my needs have changed. Once you begin creating your forms, you will be amazed at the many applications and uses you will come up with. When I was using the Italian civil birth records on microfilm, I created a chart that included, at the top, the name of the village, the microfilm roll number, and the surname of the search. Below this I created a lined form with columns to accommodate the pertinent information found on the form. This included:

- the name of the person the record was for
- the record number
- the date of the record
- the date of birth (which varies from the date of the record)
- the parents' names
- the grandparents' names
- whether the parents and grandparents are living or deceased (which is indicated in these records)
- a column for notes

Town/Village _____ Region _____ Country _____							
YEAR	**TYPE**	**CERT #**	**NAME**	**COPIED**	**SEARCHED**	**TRANSC.**	**DONE**

Vital Records Form for Foreign Country Research
If you use one form per family surname, then you will have a complete index to the records you are using.

By using this form to list all of the records pertaining to one surname, I had a complete index of all the records. I later transferred the information to the family group sheets using the parents' names to divide the families. If I ever needed to get a copy of a specific record, I had all of the information I needed on the log sheet and could go directly to it on the roll of microfilm. This is especially helpful when using foreign records. Since I was looking for my grandfather's birth record and only had questionable parents' names, I needed to look at all of the people with that surname. Once I found his actual record, I only had to look at the log sheet to determine which records were for his siblings, since the parents were already listed on the log sheet. Once I had the parents' names, I could again review the log sheet and see if any of the parents' siblings were also listed (using the grandparents' names column). The benefits of this type of form are endless.

My first foray into any new record type or index includes making a photocopy of several examples of that particular record. I then create a form that will be used to extract the data from the record. Most nineteenth- and twentieth-century records, such as naturalization records from a specific court or time frame, are typeset forms with blanks to be filled in. Creating a duplicate form speeds up the transcription process. This applies to vital record forms for the states that I frequently use. I include a master copy of these forms in the appropriate state or facility folder that pertains to those records. I then use these forms rather than write the information in a notebook. After I have recorded the information and source on the pedigree and family group sheet, I file the forms in the appropriate folder or binder.

When using naturalization or Soundex indexes that are in card format, having a card that duplicates the one used by the indexer makes recording the information simple. You can get four of these blank cards on a single sheet of paper. **I do all of the indexing first, and then go back and look at the records because more than one record may appear in the same book volume or microfilm.** I save time by looking at all of the records at once. Then, if I decide to get a photocopy of that record, I staple the index card to the document and have a complete citation to obtain the record again should I or another researcher need it. My citation is right there when I enter the data into the computer or onto the pedigree or group sheet. Another advantage to using the cards is that I can quickly see what each record is. In many cases, it becomes the abstract of the document.

Idea Generator

Timesaver

Census _____ Soundex Code _____ State _____						
Vol. _____ E.D. _____						
Head of Family _____ Sheet _____ Line _____						
color _____ month _____ year _____ age _____ birthplace_____ citizenship _____						
County _____						
City _____ Street _____ House# _____						
Name	Rel	Mo	Yr	Age	Birthplace	Citizen
1						
2						
3						
4						
5						
6						
7						
8						

Soundex Card
This card duplicates a Soundex Card, so recording information will be simple.

A USEFUL FORM YOU CAN REPRODUCE

For a full-sized blank copy of the Soundex Card, see page 125. You are free to photocopy this form for personal use.

**A USEFUL FORM
YOU CAN REPRODUCE**

For a full-sized blank copy
of the Census Overview
Form see page 126. You
are free to photocopy this
form for personal use.

Important

Research Tip

Once I have *completely* transcribed the land deed, will, or other document, I attach a copy of the typed transcription to the front of the photocopied document. This serves an important function. I can quickly review the document and its contents without having to deal with bad handwriting, a faint copy, and so on. I can also highlight names and important information on the typed transcription and not mark up the photocopy. Always include the complete citation at the top of the page including the year, volume number, page number, town, county, and state pertaining to the document.

Another custom form that I find very useful is a census overview form. This form has evolved over the last few years and has been fine-tuned to match the example you see on page 17. It is a composite of several forms that have appeared in books or been used by fellow researchers. The form includes the couples' names, dates and places of birth, date of marriage and death, as well as their parents' names at the top. Below the heading are several rows and a series of columns for specific information. Since most people will only appear in perhaps five or six consecutive federal census records as an adult, I divided the form into six wide rows. In the first column on the left, I list the years that the couple should appear in the federal census. Also included in this box is the microfilm roll number for the specific census (and/or index). The next column to the right is for listing the information I actually found on that particular census. The next column is where I have already unsuccessfully looked. Keeping track of this is, as I have said before, extremely important. If you have spent an hour unsuccessfully looking through every page of a particular town's record for a person, you don't want to do it again, do you? **Record the negative as well as the positive results!** The last column lists the actual location where the information was found, including the state, county, town, enumeration district number (when used), sheet number, line number, as well as the family visitation number. This sheet contains the entire citation for the information. All of these small pieces of information, when used together, enable me to duplicate that search in an instant. In addition, I *always* get a microfilm printout of the specific page. If the family appears at the top or bottom of the page, I will also copy the preceding or following page. This is necessary in order to get a better picture of the family's neighborhood and those who lived around them.

You will now have a form that looks like the example on page 17.

Once the information is completely entered on the census log sheet, you can file the actual photocopies and insert the log sheet into your family group sheet binder, along with the family it pertains to. **Now, with a single glance, you can see what information you found that covers a period of fifty or sixty years.** Scanning the locations where the family was found can also reveal their migration patterns. Having all of the census information on one page allows you to compare the information from one census year to the next, many times revealing errors in age or names that show up.

Blank forms, which follow the federal census formats, are readily available in many books as well as at the National Archives facilities or Family History Centers. Having a blank copy of each census year available for reference when you are looking at the actual census can help you determine

Name: _Rhodes_ BRAMAN b 24 Mar 1803 place PA m bef 1830 place _____ m _____ place _____ d aft 1870 place _____ d ca 1865 place _____ s/o Samuel & Margaret RICHTMEYER

Name: _Catherine RUSS_ b 2 Aug 1806 place _____ d/o

YEAR/ROLL #	INFORMATION FOUND	SEARCHED	FOUND IN:
1830	BRAMAN, Rhodes 1 male 20-30 y 2 females under 5 y 1 female 20-30 y 1 male 30-40 y *living next door is James BRAMAN (1 m 60-70 y & 1 f 50-60 y)		Worcester Twp. Otsego Co., NY pg 151
1840	BRAMAN, Rhodes household = 6 people 1 male under 5 y 1 female 5-10 y 1 male 30-40 y 2 females 10-15 y 1 female 30-40 y		Worcester Twp. Otsego Co., NY pg 314
1850	BRAMAN, Rhodes male 47y farmer $2200 b NY BRAMAN, Catharine fem 44y — b NY BRAMAN, Margaret fem 21y — b NY BRAMAN, Hamilton male 13y — b NY BRAMAN, Pardon O. male 20y — b NY BRAMAN, Nelson male 6y — b NY	Worcester Twp. Schoharie Co. NY Not listed	Summit Twp. Schoharie Co. NY pg 311B Lines 20-25
1860	BRAMAN, Rhodes male 58y farmer $1400/$500 all b in NY BRAMAN, C. fem 56y BRAMAN, H. male 23y BRAMAN, M. fem 34y BRAMAN, P. male 20y BRAMAN, M. fem 30y BRAMAN, Nelson male 17y BRAMAN, E. fem 25y		Berlin Twp. Wayne Co., PA pg 63 or 173 fam#1101/1101
1870	BRAMAN, Cathers fem 65y keeping house $3000 b NY WHITMORE, Maria fem 42y housekeeper — b NY BRAMAN, Pardon male 29y farmer $3000/$800 b NY BRAMAN, Betty fem 29y keeping house — b PA BRAMAN, Adie fem 3/12y — b PA		Berlin Twp. Wayne Co., PA pg 11 lines 21-25

Census Overview Form

This form gives you a composite of the information you will find for a family in the various census years. At a glance, you can see how the family evolved over each ten-year period.

what each column represents when the microfilm is difficult to read. An advantage to filling in this particular form is that it forces you to look at every piece of information contained on the original census page. Too many people only look at the names, ages, and possibly the occupation of a given person. Every census record, whether federal, state, or county, offers an amazingly large base of information. You should acquaint yourself with the columns on any census. What questions are being asked? The answer may be no more than a check or mark in a column. Reading the heading on the column can provide information that is valuable to your search. The column may ask if the person's parents were foreign born; if they could read or write; if they attended school during that year; if they were married, widowed, or single; if they owned or rented their home or farm. This provides you with an abundance of personal information regarding the family. Every column could be the clue you need to lead you to further records. Taking a few extra seconds now will save you time later.

MAPS

Another item that I classify as a form is a map of the state or locality in which you are researching. A simple map outlining the county and town borders within the state is vital to your research. Knowing where in the county the township is located can indicate other localities that you should search. If the town or county of interest is located on any border, whether a state or county border, you should always look "over the line" for additional records. Town and county borders meant very little to our ancestors. The closest church of their denomination was not always in the same town or state in which they lived. When townships bordered on state lines, many people went to the nearest town to do their business, even if it was in the neighboring state.

Tip

After I copy these maps, I take a few minutes to color in the towns where I know individuals lived. If you have more than one family in the same vicinity, you can use various colors of highlighters to indicate each family. This makes referencing the maps much faster when you need to see what towns are adjacent to the one of interest. Another interesting fact may also show up. I had two families who intermarried in Rutland County, Vermont, but could find no marriage records in either of the towns of residence. Looking at the map showed me that the two towns in question were separated by yet another town. Upon checking the town in the middle, I was able to find the records of the marriages. Being unfamiliar with the geography of an area can be a real hindrance to research.

Maps of the townships you are interested in can also be great tools. When looking at land deeds, you can pinpoint the location of the property when landmarks such as rivers, streams, and town borders are listed in the land descriptions. Quite often you can obtain, usually from the local clerk or historical society, a map that actually lists property owners at a given time in history. Vermont's popular Beers Atlases provide township maps for most counties in

Vermont, with the books divided by county. This can be very helpful in placing your ancestors' land within the town boundaries.

A wonderful book by William Thorndale and William Dollarhide, *Map Guide to the U.S. Federal Censuses 1790-1920,* contains maps showing the county boundaries as they were in each of the census years. These maps show the old county boundaries superimposed over the current lines to clearly show where a county was located for each ten-year interval. A new book by the same author, *The Census Book,* covers all facets of the U.S. federal census record. Knowing when a state was included in the records is important. I could not find a census for Wisconsin in 1830. I later learned that it was included as Michigan territory until 1840— a minor detail that made a major difference. Whenever possible, take a few minutes to read about the records of interest to your research.

Printed Source

CORRESPONDENCE LOG

Another form or log sheet you should use is a correspondence log. This is the form where you record all correspondence that pertains to your genealogical research, whether it is by regular mail, E-mail, or fax. I prefer to keep the correspondence log in a separate file, while other researchers keep it with the family group sheets or filed by surname or locality. Again, the key to getting and staying organized is to create a system that works for you.

A correspondence log should contain the following:
- request number (see below)
- date of request
- addressee's name
- information requested
- date you received a reply
- results of request, notations, etc.

A USEFUL FORM YOU CAN REPRODUCE

For a full-sized blank copy of the Correspondence Log, see page 127. You are free to photocopy this form for personal use.

The last column is used for any notations you wish to make. If the person didn't answer all of the questions asked or you need to follow up on one of the answers, you can place a reference number in the sixth column to indicate the document number for the follow-up letter.

DATE	NAME/ADDRESS	REASON FOR LETTER	RESPONSE

Correspondence Log
A form like this allows you to keep track of all your genealogy-related correspondence.

Supplies

**A USEFUL FORM
YOU CAN REPRODUCE**

For a full-sized blank copy of the Surname Overview Form, see page 128. You are free to photocopy this form for personal use.

SURNAME OVERVIEW FORM

Another custom form that I use quite often is a surname overview form. **This form is actually a purchased form called an "All-Purpose Worksheet" and is available at office supply stores, or you can create your own.** It comes in several different sizes and formats, so pick the one that works best for you. On this sheet I list a person's name in the left column and then mark the columns indicating the types of records I will be using for that project. This may include birth, marriage, death, naturalization, burial, or passenger list, depending on the research project.

Some of you might think that all of this form making and logging takes too much time and effort. Logging information onto forms can be accomplished at home in small blocks of time. It also lets you review your records. I have found that it has streamlined my research to such a degree that I have more research time than ever before. Conduct and document your research in a professional, businesslike manner. These are records which, hopefully, will be passed to future generations. Many of us have had the experience of receiving a box of "grandpa's papers" and having no idea what it pertains to or what is important among the papers. Be as persistent in your documentation and organization as you are in your research.

Once you have taken a deep breath and are ready to jump in, move on to chapter two, which details how to file all of these forms.

NAME	1900 CENSUS	1910 CENSUS	1920 CENSUS	BIRTH	MARRIAGE	DEATH	NATURAL.
IANNIZZI, Cosimo	N/A	OK	OK	N/A	OK	OK	OK
IANNIZZI, Giuseppe	N/A	N/A	OK	OK	OK	OK	N/A
NOTES							
Cosimo Bruno Iannizzi came to the U.S. in 1907 from Italy.							

Surname Overview Form
Use this form to record the records currently available for each member of a surname group.

TWO

Controlling the Paper Pile

Timesaver

Whether you are new to genealogical research or have been at it for many years, there are some problems that all researchers have faced at one time or another. Keeping track of your accumulated data is one problem that can be a hindrance to future research. If items are not properly documented, organized, filed, and retrievable when needed, they cannot provide you with the information you need to do further research. By employing certain techniques *during* your research, you can actually save time and effort in the long run. **By utilizing small blocks of time during the week or on weekends, you can organize your research files to make future research more efficient and profitable.** Being able to see what you already have will prevent you from wasting time and money by duplicating your work. Get into good habits now. No matter how long you have been researching, it is never too late to get organized and learn good habits for the future.

As most of us have discovered, when we begin researching, the paper we accumulate takes on a life of its own. It seems to breed faster than we can file it. How do we regain some semblance of control and yet still enjoy the task? Personally, I feel great when I feel organized. Every time I can lay my hands on a piece of paper I need or want, I feel a certain sense of pride in my work. I must admit that I am not always completely organized and do beat myself up at times when I cannot find something I need. But those times are fewer these days. Since my actual research time is limited, being able to easily find what I need allows me to squeeze more actual research time out of my week.

Organizational techniques that I have learned and implemented from books, my business background, and experience have streamlined my workload. Think about the different types of filing systems you have come in contact with over your lifetime. How were they organized? Always keep in mind that the term "files" does not necessarily mean a hanging file or file cabinet. Your personal telephone and address book is technically a file. It is organized alphabetically since that is how you would look up a name. You must consider how you will use a file when you need to add or retrieve something. This is where the customization of your particular file system comes in.

Some people like to keep their research strictly in surname order in a file cabinet. This works very well for most people. However, the problem of too much paper in one folder eventually creeps up. This is when you will have to adapt your system to fit your current needs. You could try dividing the folders by each generation of the surname, thereby creating family groups as subfiles of the main file. This would help create more manageable files but could also pose a new problem. By separating the files into each generation, you may have to duplicate some records for entry into both files. Always think through the possible changes and look at the pros and cons of each change.

Example: You have a file set up for the Rounds surname, which has become inefficiently large. It probably contains birth, marriage, death, land, probate, and census records, to name a few. You could divide the file into individual generations of the Rounds family. You may then be creating five or more separate files such as:

1. Orville^5 ROUNDS & Ella Mae Louise BISSONNETTE
2. Spencer^4 ROUNDS & Malona CARPENTER
3. Linus^3 ROUND & Hannah WESCOTT
4. Joseph^2 ROUND & Phebe (RENSLOW or MILLINGTON)
5. James^1 ROUND & Urana COLE

Step By Step

You now have five folders, each designating one generation from your Rounds ancestry. Now you will need to divide the records that were stored in the original Rounds surname file. The birth records of your ancestor's siblings are easy—you would file them with the parents they were born to. But what about Spencer Rounds's birth record? Will you file it with Linus and Hannah's file or in his own Spencer Rounds and Malona Carpenter file? Will you make a duplicate of the record and file it in both places? What about Spencer's marriage record? What about census records pertaining to the whole family? These are the types of questions you should ask before changing or modifying your filing system. Make some decisions regarding the way you will use the file or look something up, and then implement it across the board. As long as the entire system is consistent and you know where to find something, it will work.

In the above example, I decided to file all records pertaining to any individual *prior to his or her marriage* with the parents. From the point of marriage onward, the record was filed with the individual. For instance, Spencer Rounds's birth record and all census records with him listed as a child or an adult *prior to his marriage* to Ella Mae Louise Bissonnette were filed with his parents, Linus Round and Hannah Wescott. Spencer's marriage and death records, and the census records after his date of marriage were filed in his own folder with his wife.

Once you make this decision, maintaining the files is easy. You need to apply this rule to all of your surname files. Being consistent is the key to making a file system work. Maintaining smaller files makes them more useable and easily reviewed in a few minutes.

I would love to be able to tell you that there is one perfect filing system to use. The fact is, there isn't one. As I said before, the system will not work if it does not make sense to you or accommodate your research needs. Ease of use will determine how diligently you use the system and how efficient it will be. An elaborate system might work well on paper in the planning stages, but could be too cumbersome to put into daily use. **Thinking through how you will use the file, what items you will need to file, as well as how you would look for items that are already filed are major considerations.**

Creating and maintaining a good filing system will not happen overnight. You will occasionally find faults with any system and need to adjust it until it works flawlessly. I have finally gotten to that point in my filing. I run into fewer and fewer problems when it comes to locating any specific person or record within my system. I know what I have and what I still need. This is your goal. Start out simple and as you progress, you can, and will, alter the system to fit your current needs.

Important

DIFFERENT FILING SYSTEMS FOR DIFFERENT PROJECTS

Set up a filing system that works for you today. Easy for me to say, right? Well, we all have different styles, and your filing system must fit *your* style or it will not work, nor will you be encouraged to use it. I actually use two slightly different filing systems for my two genealogy projects.

One project is my mother's Yankee ancestry, and the second is my father's Italian immigrant ancestry. The filing system that works for the first does not necessarily work for the second. There are definitely some similarities in the two, but also many unique qualities. The basic difference is the number of files and subfiles needed to store the accumulated information. My mother's family file consists of many more documents, research logs, notes, and family group sheets than my father's family files, mainly because of the amount of available materials from the United States as compared to Italy. The Italian records available for research are usually limited to the microfilms of the civil records from the nineteenth century. The U.S. research materials are more extensive and include land, probate, court, and naturalization records, producing a lot more paper that needs to be organized. Some projects require a more elaborate filing system than others. Customize your system to fit the needs of your research project and the amount of material it contains.

To begin, you must regain control over what you already have. For some of you, that means organizing years of research that may be piled all over the place. For others, you may already have a file system that sort of works but needs to be fine-tuned. I have always found it more enjoyable to research

Tip

Tip

than to organize. If the task seems overwhelming to you right now, remember that you accumulated the paper one piece at a time, which is how you will organize it from now on—*one piece at a time.* I call this the "bushel basket approach." **You can put all those papers into one "basket" and remove them one by one. This is a great project to work on when you have just a few minutes** (see the timesaving sidebar on page 25). By approaching the task this way, it will be easier to deal with. Don't look at the whole project; just look at one part at a time. If you thought about cleaning your whole house in one day, you'd probably sit down with a cup of coffee until the thought passed. If you concentrated on one room or area at a time, it would be less daunting. The same goes for the paper you will be organizing now. Do it one piece at a time!

Organizing your files presents an opportunity to review what you already have and make sure it is well documented. Looking at and reading every item before you place it in a new file will help refresh your memory about things you researched long ago. Many times we fail to review records that we previously obtained and miss some important clues to further our research. When you originally found that census record for your great-grandparents, you didn't know great-grandma's maiden name. Now when you look at the same record with knowledge of her maiden name, you may discover another family living in the neighborhood bearing the same surname. They will most likely turn out to be her relatives. Reviewing your older records with your current knowledge can bring many surprises and rewards. This step only takes a few minutes and can result in many new discoveries.

Another bonus to reviewing your older records is that you can create a log sheet to list what you already have. This can be done on a piece of lined paper or index cards for now. As you refile the documents, make a list of what you have, breaking it down to each individual couple or family. Allocating perhaps fifteen minutes a couple of times a week to do this chore is a painless way to regain control. If you do not have a lot of records, they could simply be listed by surname. I prefer filing by each married couple using the same rules that applied when I divided the surname files: records for any individual are filed with his parents *until* his marriage, and then all of the records pertaining to that person *after* marriage are filed in his own folder. Again, applying the rules across the board will result in a very uniform filing system.

When filing copies of records (census, birth, marriage), list the subject of the record and the citation on an index card or piece of paper. Attach this note to the upper corner (I alternate the right and left upper corners to avoid bulk) of the document. By doing this, you can tell at a glance what the record is and whom it pertains to without removing the record from the file and deciphering the handwriting. If the document is a land or probate document, attach a *transcription* of the document, or at least an *abstract* of it, to the original before filing. This will enable you to scan through all of your filed documents and quickly see to whom and what it pertains. Remember that being able to efficiently file or retrieve documents is the goal.

I actually created forms, four to a page, to enter the data, and I use these for all of my records, even those with complete transcriptions. By creating

Timesaver

THINGS YOU CAN ACCOMPLISH
IF YOU HAVE SOME SPARE MINUTES
Fifteen Minutes:

1.   Assemble materials to create an alphabetical index for your pedigree charts.

2.   Review your pedigree charts for the proper formatting of information.

3.   Make a list of supplies you need for your "genealogical office."

4.   Post a query on an appropriate Internet site.

5.   Create a file folder or binder for each surname you are researching.

6.   Transcribe information to an overview form.

7.   Call or write to a facility of interest to obtain pamphlets and information about it.

8.   Read the E-newsletters you have printed from the Internet.

9.   Create a list of thoughts and ideas that occur to you regarding your genealogical research.

10.   Browse a chapter or two in a genealogical publication or book.

Thirty Minutes:

1.   Write a letter to relatives to determine what information they might have.

2.   Review your pedigree charts to see what records you still need.

3.   Draft a standard letter of inquiry for facilities and relatives.

4.   Assemble a research pencil case with all of the supplies you will need.

5.   Create a binder or tote for the facilities that you regularly use.

6.   Sort through the many records you have accumulated and check each one against your pedigree and family group sheets to determine that the information has been transferred.

7.   Make a list of the records you still need to get or items you still need to research.

Thirty Minutes on the Computer:

1.   Visit one of the many genealogical sites to determine what links they may offer.

2.   Create a general letter of inquiry for relatives or research facilities.

Timesaver

THINGS YOU CAN ACCOMPLISH
IF YOU HAVE SOME SPARE MINUTES—Continued

3. Create blank forms for record extraction, indexes, etc.

4. Enter some data into your genealogical program.

5. Transcribe a document and then create an abstract of it.

6. Review your genealogical program to see what reports and forms it will produce.

7. Visit a genealogical site with articles of educational interest to learn about a new record type.

8. Subscribe to a couple of mailing lists that pertain to the state and county of interest.

9. Utilize one of the many genealogical sites containing databases or indexes of records.

10. Search an online catalog for books or manuscripts of interest to you.

11. Print out some of the many E-newsletters of interest to read when you have a few minutes.

\di'fin\ *vb*

Definitions

Transcription—"A verbatim record or exact copy of a portion or all of some proeceedings, writings, or words"

Abstract—"Setting forth pertinent portions of a writing or document; the act of selecting pertinent portions of writing."

Source: *What Did They Mean By That? A Dictionary of Historical Terms for Genealogists* by Paul Drake.

and using a standard form, every record will be labeled equally and thoroughly. I have one form for census documents, one for vital records, one for deeds, and one for miscellaneous records that don't fit any of the previous categories. These forms are technically abstracts of the documents you are filing. You will be amazed how much faster it is to retrieve and review any document within your files by using this simple method. Each document can be labeled in a minute or so, enabling you to get several done in one of your allocated blocks of time. I also keep a folder with the forms, some documents, and a pen in my briefcase to work on when I have to wait for one of my daughters or in a doctor's office. I really dislike wasting time. If you keep some of these forms in your research notebook, you can complete them while riding on the bus or train.

The files pertaining to my father's Italian line contain fewer documents because of the limited availability of foreign records. For these files, I use a slightly different approach. I utilize sheet protectors to encapsulate each individual document (most of these documents are microfilm copies, not originals) and store them in a three-ring binder. On each sheet protector I placed a blank address label (use whatever size works for you) in the upper right corner. I have even color-coded the labels to signify whether the document pertains to my grandmother's or grandfather's line. On this label I write whom the document pertains to, what type of document it is, the date, the pedigree chart number, and the person number of the individual(s) taken from the pedigree charts. I then keep them in numerical rather than alphabetical order. By utilizing the sheet protectors, I do not have to stick the label directly to the document but still have my "synopsis" attached to it.

Sheet protectors are available in almost all office supply stores and many discount department stores. Make sure they are labeled as archival safe on the box before buying. They will protect your documents from deterioration and are always recommended for original documents as well as copies. Since acid will migrate from one document or photograph to another, always keep them encapsulated to protect the documents and any adjacent papers from premature deterioration.

Supplies

The Evolution of a Filing System

When I first started doing research, I kept all of my notes, pedigree charts, family group sheets, documents, and whatever else in one three-ring binder. Then something began to happen. My ancestors seemed to multiply faster than I could keep up with them. I had obtained copies of census records, land records, and notes from various sources. Suddenly one notebook became two, two became three, and so on. I tried to keep the families in alphabetical order. That worked for a while, but I got tired of moving the files every time another family needed to squeeze into that binder. My ancestors were moving around more than I was! As with any human beings, they kept outgrowing their current living quarters!

It was then that I realized I needed more than one type of file. I thought about how I would be using the files and retrieving information. **I decided to establish one binder for the pedigree charts, one binder for the family group sheets, and one file for copies of documents that I acquired.** Each file resides in either a three-ring binder or hanging file folder. I chose binders for the first two so the papers wouldn't float all over if I dropped it. (I only wanted to organize it once.) I chose a hanging file for the third type (copies of documents that I acquired) since I do not access them nearly as often as the other two types. I never take these documents out of my house, so there was no need to contain them in a binder. And the information should have been transferred to the pedigree and family group sheets before filing.

Tip

The first file or binder contains the pedigree charts: the forms that show your bare-bones lineage. Even this file gets large pretty fast if your research pays off. Every person has two parents, four grandparents, eight great-grandparents, and so on. When you get to the tenth generation, there are 1,024 people on the pedigree chart! That only includes your ancestors, not their siblings. Oh, how we wish we could get all of their names! I still have not gotten to the point of needing more than one binder for the pedigree charts. I print or copy both sides of the pedigree chart, creating a double-sided page and thereby carrying only half as much paper. The resulting charts then read like a book.

If you take the 1,024 people who are all responsible for you being on the earth today and figure out how many descendants they might have had, the number is staggering. If you average the number of children in each of those ten generations to five who survived, then *each* of those 512 couples (1,024 people) would have almost two million descendants. Now try to multiply that by 512, and you get an idea of how large the database/notebook could become. I know that none of us will identify all of those people, and not all families had five children (perish the thought that some had ten or more), but the realization of how quickly the numbers multiply is important at this point. It makes the need for some type of organized system a necessity, not a luxury. The sooner you get it done, the more research time you will have.

Idea Generator

My solution started with producing an alphabetical index of all my identified ancestors (this was in the precomputer programs era) that was both easy to use and portable. I came up with the idea for a file system when my daughter was reorganizing my uncle's Rolodex. **Why not create an ancestral Rolodex?** Index cards (3″ × 5″) work extremely well for this. I began with person number one on my pedigree chart number one. I wrote the surname in the upper left corner in bold capital letters. Starting at the bottom of the card (you'll see why later), I wrote the name of the last person to bear that surname; in this case, it was my mother. Since the surname ends with her, there will be no entries on the card below her. For this reason, most cards will have a female at the bottom.

Think of the card as a stairway to the past. The person at the bottom of the card stands at the bottom of the stairs, closest to you. The next line, or step, up will be her father. The next line will be his father and so on. Proceed this way until you have exhausted the surname. All the names on the card will be male except for the bottom line. Since my original pedigree chart files were on paper, I simply started on the first page and flipped through the rest until I had completed the surname, checking each one off as I went. I kept the pedigree charts and my index cards in a basket on the kitchen counter. The basket included blank index cards, a recipe card box with alphabetical dividers, pens, highlighters, sticky notes, and a notepad, along with my notebook of pedigree charts. **While I made supper, talked on the phone (or should I say, when I was on hold), I whittled away at the project.** Before I knew it, I had completed it. By keeping the materials handy, I was able to work for five minutes or longer several times each day. I also carried the basket to the family room when I was watching television. I used to cross-stitch while I "watched" TV, but that was in my pregenealogy life.

Timesaver

As I filled in the cards, I included the following information on each line (see the sample index card on page 29): the birth and death dates of the individual; and whom they married, when and where. No birth or death information is needed for the spouse as it will appear on the card bearing his or her surname.

The number (B616) that appears in the upper right corner is the Soundex code for the surname BARBER. Some of the U.S. federal census records (and other federal records) use this coding technique for the indexes in later years (1880, 1900, 1910, and 1920). Note: Not all states are indexed, and

```
BARBER                                    B616

Hoxxey, Sr. (c1767-1837) m Rhoda RUSSELL 1790 VT

Hoxey, Jr. (1791-1864) m Nancy EMERY c1812 VT/NH?

Annie Delilah (1817-1894) m/1 Joseph A. ROGERS 1839 VT

                        m/2 James HOLMES 1857 VT/NH


⊕ colored dots                    pedigree chart #3
```

not all years are complete. (See *The Census Book: A Genealogist's Guide to Federal Census Facts, Schedules and Indexes.*)

When a person marries more than once, it is a good idea to list the other spouses on the card if you know them. This can aid in your research when you find a record pertaining to your ancestor with a spouse listed other than the one you descend from. Remembering all of those names becomes impossible as you accumulate more names. I keep as little of this information in my head as possible. There is too much in there already, and as I get older, I realize that it is not a safe, or reliable, place to store information.

The card also bears the pedigree chart number that the family appears on in my binder. Think of the cards as an alphabetical index to the pedigree charts. Our ancestors were not kind enough to be born in alphabetical order, but we have to organize them this way. As you complete the cards, you can file them in alphabetical order behind the appropriate index tab in the recipe box. I strongly recommend getting a two-hole punch and punching the cards on the bottom. You can then insert individual binder rings (available in multiple sizes in most office supply or stationery stores) through the two holes. Be smart and use two rings. I started with only one, and eventually the ring sprung and I was playing three hundred-card pickup on the library floor! The rings can easily be increased in size as the file expands.

Now that you have the cards completed and in order, you can move on to your family group sheets. These are the forms on which you list not only your ancestors, but all of their children as well. As any seasoned researcher knows, it is important to know all of the children of your grandparents and whom they married. When great-grandpa or grandma dies, the other might go live with a surviving child. If you don't know who they are, whom they married, and where they lived, that search is much more difficult.

Example: One research project I had worked on was for a family in Vermont. The family had resided in Vermont for several generations and consisted of thirteen known children. Fortunately, all of the children had been documented as they married and were thoroughly recorded on the family group sheets. Suddenly, the parents, an elderly couple, just disappeared from the Vermont records around 1881 or so. No death or burial record could be found. The cemetery where many of the family were interred

Case Study

was checked and no gravestone was present for either the man or woman.

The next step was to check the probate and land records to see if the couple sold their land or willed it to one of the surviving children. There was only one land transaction that had occurred before the elderly couple disappeared, which listed several of the children and their places of residence. The places of residence matched up with those already recorded with only one new piece of information. That piece of information was the one I needed. It indicated that one daughter, after her marriage, had moved to San Francisco, California, with her husband, who was a whaling boat captain. A quick check of the 1900 California census index showed the elderly couple living with this daughter in San Francisco.

Subsequent research yielded their death records in California as well as a large article on the front page of the San Francisco newspaper chronicling the family and its history back five generations. The article was very extensive and accurate. The headline read, "Woman dies leaving 108 descendants, 6 grandsons to be pallbearers." This was highly unusual for the very early 1900s when death notices for women were almost nonexistent. Remember, this was found as a result of keeping copious records on all of the family members.

As I stated earlier, I began by keeping the family group sheets in binders, divided into alphabetical order by surname. I still do that, but now they fill more than twenty binders. Since I got very tired, and jealous, of all the moving around they were doing, I decided to fill one binder and then begin another. **Color-coding these binders enables me to quickly locate records.** I started using different-color binders but quickly realized that there was not a large variety of colors available, unless you want expensive binders. Being the frugal New Englander that I am (it's hard to get away from those roots), I purchased two packages of colored dots at the stationery store. They came in primary colors in two sizes. I bought the larger size for the binders and the smaller size for the index cards. I am still on my first packages after all these years—a small investment that really paid off.

Tip

I purchase inexpensive binders at a discount store whenever they have a sale (usually during the back-to-school sales) and then fill them as needed. These binders never leave my house, so I don't care what they look like. If you have to store yours somewhere visible, you might want to stick with one color and brand so they look nicer. I put the large dots on the binder spine to identify the notebook, and the small dots on the divider tabs that separate the families contained within the binder, to identify their "home place." All of the families in the red dot binder bear a red dot on the dividers. This takes only a few minutes to accomplish.

By doing this, I can remove whatever families I want to take on a research trip, put them into a traveling binder, and still know which binder to return them to. I find that when I get home, the research must wait until I can catch up on laundry, family, or whatever needs my attention. By having every divider "dotted," it can sit for weeks and I'll still know where to refile it. I simply open the red dot binder and insert the family back in alphabetical order. It is easy to see if a file is in the wrong binder since the dots are clearly visible on the tabs.

Another small dot is placed on the index card pertaining to the family included in that binder. This way I can use the index cards like a true Rolodex file, easily locating any person or family in both the pedigree charts and family group sheet binders. Even though I only take selected families with me on any given research trip, my index cards are always with me. This solves the problem of coming across a familiar name that I may not have been looking for, and not being able to remember the particulars on that person. Another benefit of using the cards became clear when I was researching at a facility that would not allow notebooks or briefcases in the research room. After showing the cards to the attendant, I was allowed to take them in with me. The reason for these restrictions is due to loss from theft or someone accidentally picking up loose papers along with their notes. It has happened several times in different facilities, so restrictions are sometimes required. The note cards, however, are small enough that nothing can be hidden in them, and they don't always face the same restrictions.

The last portion of this filing system addresses what to do with the copies of documents you will accumulate. First, I do not get a copy of every single record I find, with the exception of census, land, and probate records. The cost of copies of vital records, whether certified or not, can become prohibitive. I will, however, print copies from microfilm when allowed. Microfilm printouts are usually very reasonable and cheap insurance against mistakes in transcription.

When you purchase a copy of a vital record from the town clerk or state agency, and sometimes you will be required to, realize that most town clerks will fill in their own form with information from the original record book. Rarely will you get a photocopy of the record since they were usually recorded in large ledger books, and your record is only one or two lines on the entire page. Keeping in mind that not every form was created equally, not all information included in the original record will fit on the "standard form" the office uses. Many times there are small notations contained in the record that do not have a corresponding line on the form. The clerk will also be reading from the original record and then transferring the information to the form. **You are therefore paying for a certified copy of *someone else's interpretation of the record*.** I have actually obtained certified copies, by mail, that included incorrect information. Upon reviewing the record in person later, it became clear that the clerk did not use sufficient care in her transcription, or pertinent information was left off the record I received. This is especially true of many death certificates. Several times the name of the informant (the person who gave the information for the record) is left off the filled-in form. This piece of information is important to the genealogist, as it assists in determining how accurate the information is. Other times I have found locations incorrectly listed.

Example: A death certificate from the state of Maine incorrectly listed the deceased's place of birth incorrectly as Canton, Maine, instead of Canton,

Warning

Case Study

\di'fin\ *vb*

Definitions

Ahnentafel—German for ancestor table or chart, which consists of a standard numbering system. The first person on the chart is number one, the person's father is number two, and the mother is number three. The chart numbering continues in the following pattern: any person's father is double his/her number and the mother's number is double plus one. An individual's grandparents would then be number four, five, six, and seven with the males being even numbers and all females being odd numbers.

Massachusetts. I now have a certified copy of an incorrect record. Think of the confusion this results in for anyone else looking at that record years from now.

If you do not have very many documents, you can file them behind the family group sheets in your color-coded binders. This can get cumbersome when you take the "family" out and put it in the traveling binder. If you have transcribed and documented the information from the records to your pedigree and family group sheets, you don't need to have the document with you. By filing it separately, you can easily access it but not be encumbered with extra paper when on research trips.

I maintain additional files marked "records" in which I file these copies. As I stated before, I actually have two slightly different files. One is maintained by surname and then by couple, while the other is filed by pedigree chart number. In the upper right corner of the copy, I note the pedigree chart number and person number, such as 7/4. Example: Spencer Rounds and his wife Malona Carpenter are persons number 4 and 5 on chart number 7. The 7/4 indicates to me that the record pertains to chart #7 and person #4 (Spencer Rounds). If you use an ahnentafel (see the definition at left) numbering system, you would place the ahnentafel number on the record instead. Since you will have documents pertaining to collateral ancestors (siblings without a pedigree chart or ahnentafel number), designate them with a letter following their parents' or spouses' designation, such as 7/4a or 7/5b, depending on their position in the family. So records pertaining to the children of Spencer and Malona Rounds will bear the notation 7/4&5a, with 4 and 5 representing the couple. If the record pertains to two people, such as the marriage of Spencer Rounds and Malona Carpenter, I designate it by writing 7/4&5. I then file these in numerical order. I can easily find any document by looking at my index cards to determine the pedigree chart number, and then referring to the pedigree charts—a quick two-step process.

The other file, the one by surname, will have every document pertaining to one couple and all of their children contained within it. Only the child who is the ancestor will have his own file after he marries.

COMPUTER FILING SYSTEMS

The only problem with the previous system stems from the use of computer programs that do not assign numbers for chart continuations, unless you have the record to carry over. (See chart on page 34.) Because of this, every time you obtain a new generation or two, the printout of the charts will be numbered differently than the previous batch. With the ahnentafel system, every individual in your ancestry has a specific number assigned to him or her, regardless of whether you know their name or not. This number will never change, unlike the chart numbering system. Since I have the old handwritten charts, which I manually (and correctly) numbered years ago, I only use these numbers and disregard the ones on computer-generated charts.

Ahnentafel of Shirley Diana ROGERS

1 Shirley Diana ROGERS (1926-living)

2 Seneca Baker ROGERS (1885-1959)
3 Diana Belle ROUNDS (1892-1941)

4 Constant Hoxey ROGERS (1842-1929)
5 Teressa Rebecca STEARNS/EMERY (1847-1924)
6 Orville ROUNDS (1871-1948)
7 Elle Mae BISSONETT (1869-1954)

8 Joseph A. ROGERS (1813-1853)
9 Anna Delilah BARBER (1817-1894)
10 Harvey STEARNS (1800-1853)
11 Rebecca BROWN (1804-1864)
12 Spencer ROUNDS (1823-1906)
13 Malona CARPENTER (1840-1888)
14 Ambrose BISSONETT, Jr. (1834-1877)
15 Celinde "Mary" ACKEY/ACHE (1842-1871)

16 Constant ROGERS (1786- ?)
17 Love Sanborn CUMMINGS (1788- ?)
18 Hoxey BARBER, Jr. (1791-1864)
19 Nancy EMERY (1793-1850)
20 Deacon Ephraim STEARNS (1755-1843)
21 Mary/Molly GILMAN (1760-1850)
22 Jacob BROWN (1780-1849)
23 Joanna HOUGHTON (1783-1852)
24 Linus ROUND (ca 1798-1875)
25 Hannah WESCOT (ca 1795-1874)
26 Calvin D. CARPENTER (1814-1887)
27 Melona SUMNER (1806-1841)
28 Ambrose BISSONETT, Sr. (1805-1893)
29 Marie Josephte LUSSIER (ca 1810-1885)
30 Francis AKIE/ACHE (ca 1810- ?)
31 Louisa/Mary STRAIGHT (ca 1824- ?)

32 Samuel ROGERS (1748-1811)
33 Mehitable HUBBARD (1752-1840)
34 Solomon CUMMINGS (1743-1802)
35 Mary/Molly GRAHAM (1752-1817)
36 Hoxxey BARBER, Sr. (ca 1767-1837)
37 Rhoda RUSSELL (1770-1813)
38 Captain Daniel EMERY (1757-1825)
39 Hanna BATES (1765-1852)
40 Moses STEARNS (1728-1808)
41 Ruth HOUGHTON (1732-1815)
42 Constantine GILMAN (1723-1802)
43 Mehitable (?) (ca (1734-1764)
44 Joseph BROWN (1743-1816)
45 Mary EATON (1741-1816)
46 Oliver HOUGHTON (1733/4-1790)
47 Rebecca HOLT (1758-1844)
48 Joseph ROUND (1775-1831)
49 Phebe MILLINGTON or RENSLOW (ca 1789-after 1850)
50 Johnson WESCOTT (ca 1758-1828)
51 Rhoda SIMONDS (ca 1776-1849)
52 John CARPENTER (1774-1846)
53 Druzilla NICHOLS (ca 1783-1852)
54 Henry George SUMNER (1771-1856)
55 Sarah HALL (1779-1855)
56 Michel BISSONETT (1766- ?)
57 Marie Angeline LANGEVIN (ca 1780- ?)
58 Joseph LUSSIER (? - ?)
59 Marie Josette OUILLIAM (? - ?)
60 unknown
61 unknown
62 unknown
63 unknown

Tip

The only way that I have found, thus far, to avoid the problem of numbering on printouts is to fill in the blanks with "unknown." The computer program does not know that it is not a "name" but only knows that there is information in the field, and treats it like a person, thereby numbering the chart to continue in sequential order. (See chart on page 35.) Hopefully, in the near future, the genealogical computer software creators will correct this oversight.

Most computer programs allow you to generate an alphabetical index of the names in their database with a simple click of a button. This may be an easy task; however, every time you add new people, you must reprint the

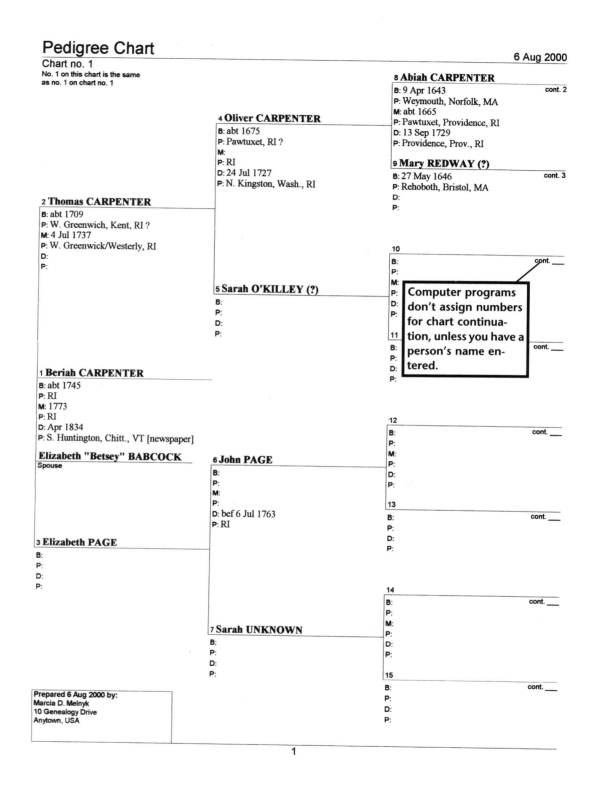

Pedigree Chart

Chart no. 1
No. 1 on this chart is the same
as no. 1 on chart no. 1

6 Aug 2000

8 Abiah CARPENTER
cont. 2
B: 9 Apr 1643
P: Weymouth, Norfolk, MA
M: abt 1665
P: Pawtuxet, Providence, RI
D: 13 Sep 1729
P: Providence, Prov., RI

4 Oliver CARPENTER
B: abt 1675
P: Pawtuxet, RI ?
M:
P: RI
D: 24 Jul 1727
P: N. Kingston, Wash., RI

9 Mary REDWAY (?)
cont. 3
B: 27 May 1646
P: Rehoboth, Bristol, MA
D:
P:

2 Thomas CARPENTER
B: abt 1709
P: W. Greenwich, Kent, RI ?
M: 4 Jul 1737
P: W. Greenwick/Westerly, RI
D:
P:

10
cont. ___
B:
P:
M:
P:
D:
P:

5 Sarah O'KILLEY (?)
B:
P:
D:
P:

Computer programs don't assign numbers for chart continuation, unless you have a person's name entered.

11
cont. ___
B:
P:
D:
P:

1 Beriah CARPENTER
B: abt 1745
P: RI
M: 1773
P: RI
D: Apr 1834
P: S. Huntington, Chitt., VT [newspaper]

Elizabeth "Betsey" BABCOCK
Spouse

12
cont. ___
B:
P:
M:
P:
D:
P:

6 John PAGE
B:
P:
M:
P:
D: bef 6 Jul 1763
P: RI

13
cont. ___
B:
P:
D:
P:

3 Elizabeth PAGE
B:
P:
D:
P:

14
cont. ___
B:
P:
M:
P:
D:
P:

7 Sarah UNKNOWN
B:
P:
D:
P:

15
cont. ___
B:
P:
D:
P:

Prepared 6 Aug 2000 by:
Marcia D. Melnyk
10 Genealogy Drive
Anytown, USA

1

list. By using the index cards, you can make notes on the backs of the cards, next to the names, that you cannot and would not want to redo with every new list. Most computer-generated lists contain all names within a specified database. They do not necessarily show the lineage of one surname or the

Pedigree Chart

6 Aug 2000

Chart no. 1
No. 1 on this chart is the same
as no. 1 on chart no. 1

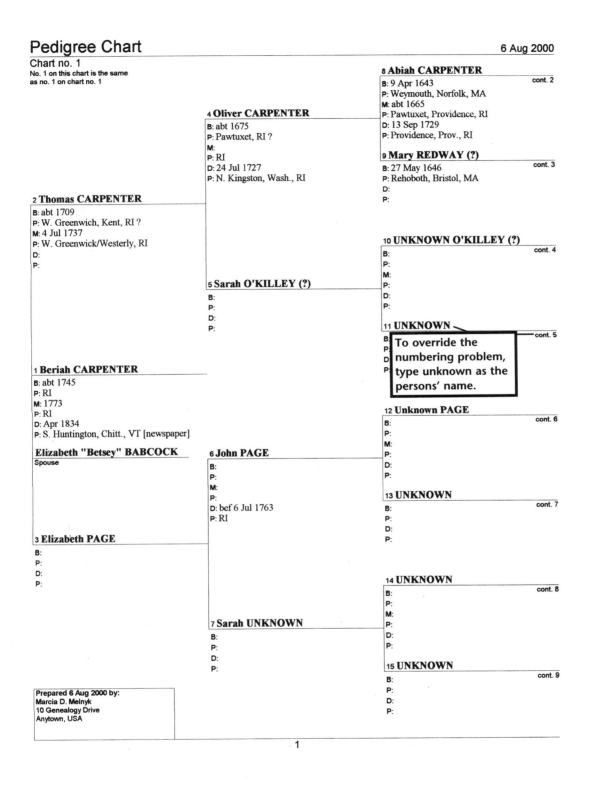

8 Abiah CARPENTER   cont. 2
B: 9 Apr 1643
P: Weymouth, Norfolk, MA
M: abt 1665
P: Pawtuxet, Providence, RI
D: 13 Sep 1729
P: Providence, Prov., RI

4 Oliver CARPENTER
B: abt 1675
P: Pawtuxet, RI ?
M:
P: RI
D: 24 Jul 1727
P: N. Kingston, Wash., RI

9 Mary REDWAY (?)   cont. 3
B: 27 May 1646
P: Rehoboth, Bristol, MA
D:
P:

2 Thomas CARPENTER
B: abt 1709
P: W. Greenwich, Kent, RI ?
M: 4 Jul 1737
P: W. Greenwick/Westerly, RI
D:
P:

10 UNKNOWN O'KILLEY (?)   cont. 4
B:
P:
M:
P:
D:
P:

5 Sarah O'KILLEY (?)
B:
P:
D:
P:

11 UNKNOWN   cont. 5
B:
P:
D:
P:

To override the numbering problem, type unknown as the persons' name.

1 Beriah CARPENTER
B: abt 1745
P: RI
M: 1773
P: RI
D: Apr 1834
P: S. Huntington, Chitt., VT [newspaper]

12 Unknown PAGE   cont. 6
B:
P:
M:
P:
D:
P:

Elizabeth "Betsey" BABCOCK
Spouse

6 John PAGE
B:
P:
M:
P:
D: bef 6 Jul 1763
P: RI

13 UNKNOWN   cont. 7
B:
P:
D:
P:

3 Elizabeth PAGE
B:
P:
D:
P:

14 UNKNOWN   cont. 8
B:
P:
M:
P:
D:
P:

7 Sarah UNKNOWN
B:
P:
D:
P:

15 UNKNOWN   cont. 9
B:
P:
D:
P:

Prepared 6 Aug 2000 by:
Marcia D. Melnyk
10 Genealogy Drive
Anytown, USA

1

relationships between individuals. The cards, including only the lineage, are a far more manageable size. I have yet to find a program that will print the information in the same way that I record it on the cards. Just the facts, ma'am, just the facts. The portability, size, and ease of use still outweigh the time spent creating the cards.

As I stated before, I have two different research projects and the filing systems for them vary in several respects. I keep my mother's and father's ancestry in separate binders since I do not research the two families at the same facilities very often. By keeping the pedigree charts and family group sheets in just one binder (for my father's ancestry), I have everything I need to take with me in one place. A second binder holds the documents I have obtained sorted by pedigree chart number and person number. I still create a set of index cards for his Italian line using the same system as before. By splitting the two families this way, I can share all of my research with cousins on either side of the family. My pedigree charts for my mother's Yankee ancestry applies to all twenty of my first cousins simply by replacing my mother's name with one of her three sisters' names. The same goes for my father's ancestry. Again, thinking through the way you will use the files will help you determine the most efficient format.

Within my mothers' ancestry is a large group of French-Canadian ancestors. Some of these lines consist of ten or more generations. Since I use specific research facilities for these records, I have created separate binders and files to accommodate them. Only the records pertaining to Canadian research are kept in these files. From the time they arrive in Vermont, the records are kept with the Yankee ancestry. I have a separate set of index cards for them as well.

Important

As you can see, there are many variations on my basic filing system, but **consistency is the key ingredient to maintaining organization.** By separating the Yankee, Italian, and French-Canadian portions of the family, I have been able to customize each of these files to fit my research needs. Since I use the same materials, binders, index cards, and hanging files for all three, I can store them in the same place, making sure that the binders are clearly marked.

Supplies

To review: **The following supplies were used in the above mentioned system:**
- binders (three-ring, 1″ to 1½″ work best and are the least expensive)
- dividers for three-ring binders, with tabs
- lined index cards (either 3″ × 5″ or 4″ × 6″)
- package of large, self-sticking, multicolored dots (to go on the binder spines)
- package of small, self-sticking multicolored dots (to go on the dividers and cards)
- hanging file folders with tabs
- file box or cabinet
- two-hole punch for punching index cards
- binder rings for the index cards
- acid-free sheet protectors

THREE

Gathering Information by Mail

Timesaver

W hy not let the U.S. Postal Service work for you? **Requesting information and records by mail can save you hours of research time.** If documents are available by mail, why spend precious time looking them up yourself? Preserve those valuable research hours for the items that are not indexed or available by mail. If you need only one document from a location, taking a trip to obtain it is not worthwhile unless you can combine it with other research or visits. On the other hand, if you need multiple documents from one facility or need to research in more than one facility in that geographical area, perhaps your time is better spent looking up the documents yourself.

Using the mail to send for information on a particular facility is a more efficient use of your time. By knowing what the repository has and does not have can save you a trip. Have the records been indexed? Are the indexes readily available? What is the cost of requesting copies of the documents? Can the documents be photocopied and mailed to you? Do you need the complete citation to obtain it by mail, or is the cost the same whether you have the complete citation or not? What form of payment is required? Do they accept faxed or E-mailed requests? (Many do not.) These are just a few of the questions you need to ask before you visit or request documents from any facility.

Before you start mailing for information or documents, create a form called a correspondence log. This form was explained in chapter one. Assign a number to every piece of correspondence you send, whether by regular mail, fax, or E-mail. Then write the number from your log directly on the response, and you will always have the question(s) you asked cross-referenced. You will be surprised how many times you will forget exactly what you asked for, and not all respondents will include your original request in their reply. File the response, along with a copy of the original request letter, in numerical order, using this reference number to indicate on your pedigree chart where the information came from, along with the complete citation. I actually keep my original request letters on a computer disk, as well as on my hard drive, using the correspondence log number as the file name. Remember that unless you receive a photocopy of the original document, you are depending on a transcription of someone else's interpretation of the record.

Reminder

Some other things to keep in mind when making a request, whether by mail, fax, or electronically, are:

- Keep your request brief and to the point.
- Include information regarding any spelling variations that may affect the search. Most clerks will only look the name up the way you have spelled it in your request.
- Do not ask for more than two records in a single correspondence.
- *Always* include a self-addressed stamped envelope (SASE) for the reply.
- Be polite and businesslike in all correspondence.
- Include your return address on *both* the envelope and letter, even though you include an SASE. Many times the mailing envelope becomes separated from the request and the recipient cannot respond to you without an address.
- Include payment, if it is required, along with your letter. Always offer to pay for the information. If the information comes from a church, a monetary donation is always a nice gesture.
- Be sure to note any enclosures included with your request, for example, copies of documents or self-addressed stamped envelope.
- Include your E-mail address, if you have one, and phone or fax number on your correspondence. It will save immeasurable time if any clarification is needed on your request. It is faster than the recipient having to write a letter to ask you a simple question or inform you that you need to provide more information, payment, and so on.
- Be patient. Responses may take several weeks (and sometimes months for overseas requests) to arrive. (See letter on page 39.)

Important

You should review your correspondence log on a regular basis to see what is still outstanding. I check mine on the first and fifteenth of the month. If the inquiry is more than two months old, I may call or write the facility to be sure the initial request was received. If the original was not received, ask if you may send another copy to a specific person's attention. This will give you one person to contact should the second request also be misplaced or not answered. It is important to keep a copy of the request in your file so you know what you have already requested. It also speeds up the process when you must send another copy. Many times you can then fax or E-mail the follow-up request.

The types of records that you may need to write for are those contained in the town or county's records office, probate or land office, historical or genealogical society, or information from relatives. Always keep in mind that the less information you ask for in each request, the more likely your

20 Nov 2000

Smithville Town Clerk
26 Main Street
Anytown, USA

Dear Town Clerk,

I am interested in obtaining a marriage record for the following persons:

> John J. Rogers, b about 1870 in Vermont, son of Joseph and
> Hannah Rogers

> Martha B. Smith, b 1872 in Connecticut, daughter of Ezekial and
> Thankful Smith

The marriage would have taken place about 1890 as their first child, James Rogers, was born in Smithville in June 1892.

I am enclosing a self-addressed stamped envelope for your reply. Please advise me of the cost for a copy of the document, which I need for a family history project. I do not need a certified copy unless that is the only type available.

If you have any questions or need any clarification, I can be reached at 999-555-1111 or by E-mail at <mbsmith@aaa.com>.

Thank you for your cooperation.

Sincerely,

Marie B. Smith
10 Genealogy Drive
Anytown, USA

Enclosure: SASE

Sample Letter to Request Information

reply will be prompt. If you think about which correspondence you take care of first, isn't it usually the ones that are easiest to complete? Overwhelming the recipient with too many questions is one sure way to be ignored.

LOOKING FOR INDEXES

Before requesting records from any local, county, or state official, check to see if there are any published indexes to the records. Many times you can initially write to the record facility to ask for copies of certain indexes by surname or time frame. If this request can be honored, you can peruse the

Timesaver

indexes yourself and will be more likely to pick up on spelling variations that the clerk may not notice. Many land, probate, and vital records have been indexed and filmed, either by the Family History Library, state societies, or other official agencies. **Using the published indexes will enable you to request specific documents by volume, page number, and so on.** This will ensure that you get the exact document you need. Citing the exact volume and page, along with the name(s) that the document pertains to, usually results in a faster response as well. Listing the name is an important addition. If you have made a mistake in the citation, the clerk can clearly see that the document pertains to someone else. The clerk may then go back to the index to get the correct citation. You would not want to anxiously open the envelope only to be disappointed to find that they sent exactly what you asked for—the wrong record! Trust me—I've done it! Some of the old books are in bad condition, and the page numbers might be unclear. Stating the name of the person the record pertains to is an alternate means of identifying the correct document. Maybe the books were in better condition when the indexes were made than they currently are. Cover your bases and include the information.

Land indexes are often recorded in two formats. One is the grantor (or seller's) index and the other is the grantee (or buyer's) index. Look at both, as you may begin to see some patterns developing. If your subject of interest is buying and selling land to and from people with the same surname, check out all of these deeds. Early land deeds will many times list the place of origin of the buyer and seller. This can be a valuable clue to migration patterns for your ancestor.

When probate records for the individual are not available, or the person died intestate (without a will), you must look to see if he distributed his property before his death. This may appear in the land records, leaving nothing to distribute in the administration of the estate. Several times I have been able to correctly narrow down the date of death by looking at all of the land deeds of the person in question. In one instance, all of the individual's land transactions seemed to be bunched together in mid-1850 with many deeds to family members. Upon further research, I finally found his gravestone and his date of death, which was 1856. He had indeed divested himself of all his land holdings in his final year of life. This was apparent by looking at the deed indexes. All of the transactions were grouped together in the indexes, both grantee and grantor. In several cases, he bought a piece of land from one son and then sold it to another son, possibly to combine certain plots to more evenly distribute them. This would not have been as apparent if I had only looked at the grantor index.

Once you have thoroughly looked at the indexes, decide if the number of documents warrants a trip to the facility. If there are more than a few, it might be more cost and time effective to obtain them yourself. Otherwise, order them by mail. Cost should also be a factor. If the copies cost the same whether you go to the facility or order them by mail with only a postage fee added, then save your time. Be aware that some facilities add a handling charge for each

Money Saver

request you make, and it can add up quickly if you are not careful. You should also be sure it is the correct document before spending your money on it. Using the microfilmed indexes and records can save money and time, especially if you are dealing with a fairly common name.

REFERENCE GUIDES FOR CORRESPONDENCE

There are several published books that can be consulted to learn what is required and where to write for certain types of records. One such book is *The Genealogist's Address Book,* by Elizabeth Petty Bentley, which is also available in CD-ROM format. It lists many organizations and institutions across the United States, classified by subject, is cross-referenced, and well indexed. Each entry includes names, addresses, telephone numbers, contact persons, and business hours for the following: libraries and archives, genealogical and historical societies, vital records offices and government agencies, surname registries, special interest groups, periodicals and newspapers, as well as publishers and booksellers.

Sources

Doing a thorough search of this book, determining what societies and organizations exist, and then utilizing these groups can be an important resource. Look up your state of interest and check each individual listing. Focus on the statewide, county, and local associations and societies. Concentrate your correspondence to the counties or towns where your ancestors lived. There are knowledgeable people within all of these organizations who can further your research in many ways. After you have determined what historical and genealogical societies to correspond with, be sure to look at the back of the book to locate religious and ethnic societies as well. How many "groups" does your ancestor belong to? Do not overlook any specialized group. Most of our ancestors fit into several groups, whether ethnic, religious, or regional. There are also listings for lineage, hereditary, and patriotic societies that your ancestor may have belonged to.

Another list that Bentley provides is one for newspaper columns in various parts of the country. Consider writing a query to post in one of these columns or perhaps place an ad in a local newspaper looking for other living descendants. Many smaller newspapers publish human-interest stories, including social columns. These small publications depend on their circulation to sell advertising space. The more people they mention in the paper, the more copies they will sell. This is especially true of the many ethnic newspapers of the early twentieth century. When I was in my early twenties, I went to visit a friend's family in Nebraska. The small, hometown newspaper mentioned my arrival, with whom I visited, and when I left. Then, after my return home, it contained an article about my trip and how much I had enjoyed it.

Bentley also includes lists of publishers, periodicals, newsletters, adoption registries, search groups, information centers, computer interest groups, and surname registries that are of interest to many researchers. The possibilities for correspondence are almost endless when you consider the options that

Printed Source

are available. Use as many as possible and let the information come to you.

Another great book is Bentley's *County Courthouse Book*. It features more than three thousand county jurisdictions and fifteen hundred New England towns and independent Virginia cities. It provides addresses, phone numbers, information about the records held, and advice about what services are offered to researchers. Corresponding with these facilities can give you a much better view of their holdings, how the records were created and recorded, and what is available to be researched. This book provides information regarding who to contact at the facility. By knowing which department or person handles the records of interest, you can speed up your reply. Again, do your homework before tackling a new location or record type.

The International Vital Records Handbook, by Thomas Jay Kemp, and other such books provide information on obtaining copies of vital records from every locality in the world, including all fifty states. Blank forms are provided that you can copy, complete, and mail to the appropriate facility. Each jurisdiction (state or country) has its own unique form, enabling you to provide all of the needed information before mailing the request. Addresses and costs are also given, although these can and will change after the publication of the book. By utilizing the "official" form, your request will usually be responded to more speedily since the information is clear and concise.

Many other books pertaining to specific topics such as naturalization or land records also include addresses and information about the records themselves and how to obtain them. Look for books that are specific to the topic you are interested in, be it a particular ethnic group, country, or record type. These books will provide you with the best information and advise you on that particular subject. Each specialized subject or area has its own peculiarities regarding records and research. Explanations and instruction in the use of the specific records will save you many frustrating hours. Books covering records for foreign countries, ethnic, or religious groups, and specific regions of the country will provide you with additional places you can write to to gather information and records for your ancestors. Books such as these are fairly plentiful today and many can be found in the reference section of your library, especially if it has a genealogical collection, or for purchase on the Internet.

UTILIZING LOCAL HISTORICAL AND GENEALOGICAL SOCIETIES

Money Saver

One organization that you should correspond with is the historical or genealogical society in your research area. I have found that many have memberships, which include free searches of their records. **You may be able to "swap" research time with someone living in that area.** This is especially true if you live in an area that has records that one of their members might need. I have had good luck in this regard since I live in New England. If you live near a National Archives facility, you could do searches of the U.S. federal census records in exchange for a search of their records. You will then save time two ways. First, they may be more familiar with the records in their area and be able to search them more quickly; and second, it may save you a trip to a remote location. Travel time should be considered when weighing the decision to travel or write for information. I always prefer to travel to the location, but even I must concede that it is not always possible, nor the best use of my time and money.

The society or organization may be interested in copies of the information you have accumulated to share with others researching families in the area. Since you wrote to them regarding residents of their town or county, other researchers will do the same. Perhaps this will result in making contact with relatives or descendants of your ancestor. I have found that most organizations, if asked in advance, are glad to have the information you can provide. Some may not have space for such documents but can usually give you references of other groups who may be interested. This is also a wonderful place to donate copies of photographs of residents, buildings, or local events. I wrote to one historical society in the Midwest on behalf of a client. I asked about a resident of the county at the turn of the century. Not only did I receive a reply, including a photocopy of a document, but the secretary passed my letter along to another descendant of the family, who turned out to have a treasure trove of information for the client. They have since visited with each other and established a wonderful friendship, all because of a simple inquiry letter that took less than fifteen minutes to compose.

I actually had a case where I requested information from a historical society in Michigan, and a letter arrived asking if I would be willing to do an equal number of hours of research for them in Massachusetts. I agreed and my prepayment check for their research time was returned to me along with a letter outlining the information the person was looking for. I was amazed to find that the research she had requested proved that we were distant cousins through one of my mother's ancestors. I did three hours of research for her, saved myself the time of traveling to Michigan to get the records, and found a cousin in the deal! The records I received from Michigan were useful to my research and had not been microfilmed.

If you cannot find a genealogical society included in one of the many books listing such facilities for your research area, try contacting the state historical or genealogical society. Another source is the town or county public library. I have found that most of these small libraries are aware of the local groups that may be small and not listed in books. The librarian or town clerk may also be able to give you the name of the most knowledgeable resident when it comes to the history of the area.

On one of my early trips to New Hampshire, I asked the librarian at the library about the history of the town. She said that she had only recently moved there, but a Mr. Smith, who lived in the brick house next to the drug store, was really knowledgeable in town history. I decided to go knock on his door and ask him a few questions. He not only knew the town's history, including stories about several of my "families," but also had copies of the

For More Info

town history book for purchase. I had never seen this book before and it proved very useful in my research.

There are many societies and organizations listed on the Internet, which will be discussed more thoroughly in chapter four. Discovering what state, county, and local genealogical or historical societies exist is far easier than ever before. With the many how-to books, directories, and address books available, as well as the ever-growing Internet community, it should be relatively easy to keep yourself busy writing letters for quite some time. Remember to keep track of them all!

CORRESPONDING WITH RELATIVES

Correspondence with other relatives should be a big part of your initial research. It is important to question older relatives regarding ancestors who were living during their lifetime. A good time to do this is around the holidays when relatives may be visiting or gathering for celebrations. If you cannot, for whatever reason, do this in person, construct a letter including some questions that you would like to ask the individual(s). As when writing to any facility, always include a self-addressed stamped envelope. If writing a response will be difficult for the person, due to poor eyesight, arthritis, or some other reason, consider calling them after they have had time to think about the questions for a while. By keeping a copy of the questions, you can ask the person one question at a time, and record the responses. Multiple conversations can yield additional information and only take a small amount of your time, perhaps in the evening or on weekends. Once you start the memory recovery process, it is amazing what can be learned. Remember to be patient and not overwhelm the person with too many questions at first.

Additionally, you should write to relatives who may have family Bibles, papers, photographs, or letters from your common ancestors. Inquire as to what they might have, and offer to send them money to make or obtain photocopies for you. Most will comply, although it may take several requests before you get results. **Remember that not everyone is as excited about the family tree as you are.** Some people will become possessive of what they have, while others will allow you to take certain items, make copies, and then return them. Another way to obtain copies is through the use of a computer scanner. If you have a laptop computer, or the person you visit has a computer and scanner, any pictures or documents can be scanned and saved on a disk or your hard drive and printed out later. With the many inexpensive, compact scanners on the market today, items can be shared more readily.

Warning

Photographs are easily duplicated at minimal cost. Having a new negative made from an old photograph is pretty easy. When you have a new negative made, it is like buying insurance for the photograph. Anything that is one-of-a-kind is subject to loss or destruction. Copies can also be made on color laser copy machines at a copy shop. I always do a color photocopy, even if the picture is black and white, since most of the older photographs have some sepia or brown tones in them. This way the copy will be aged to perfection, just like the original. I have also found that making a color copy enables me to enlarge the photo or frame the copy for display without worrying about the original fading from the sunlight. Sharing some of your unique photographs or documents with other family members might encourage them to do the same.

You can also send letters, accompanied by family group sheets, to your relatives so they can provide information on their particular family for inclusion into the family database. Remember to explain how to fill it in properly, or include a sample form. These forms are pretty confusing to the nongenealogists. All of this information will be beneficial to whoever picks up where you leave off. Think of how hard it will be for the next generation to keep track of all the relatives, now that we are such a mobile society. Will they know which state to look for records of your children or cousins? Accumulating this information now will ensure that it is even recorded at all.

WAYS TO LET INFORMATION COME TO YOU

1. Post queries on mailing lists.

2. Join a society or organization specializing in your research interests.

3. Mail questionnaires to family members and facilities that may have information.

4. Subscribe to a genealogical or historical publication.

5. Forward your information to one of the many facilities or Internet databases for posting.

6. Leave copies of your research as well as contact information in research facilities.

7. Order copies of documents or books by mail.

8. Put your name on the many genealogical and historical catalog lists.

9. Submit your data for publication in newsletters of relevance.

10. Subscribe to mailing lists on the Internet for surnames, localities, and research interests.

Technique

FINDING OUT ABOUT RESEARCH FACILITIES

Letters should not only be used when you are requesting records, but when you wish to visit a facility for research purposes. (See letter on page 46.) By writing ahead and asking for the hours, restrictions, and costs, you will be

19 Oct 2000

Vermont Historical Society Library
109 State Street
Montpelier, VT 05609

Re: Research visit in December 2000

Dear Library Staff,

I am interested in visiting the Vermont Historical Society Library the week of December 4–8, 2000. I understand that the library is closed on Mondays and open on Saturdays.

If possible, I would like the following information:

1. Are there any scheduled closings during the week that would make research impossible?

2. What are the research hours for Tuesday through Saturday of that week?

3. Are the books on open stacks or must they be paged by staff?

4. Are there any restrictions, especially for nonmembers, to access any of the collections?

5. Are laptop computers allowed in the research room?

6. Are photocopies done by the researcher or by the staff?

7. Is there public parking, either on the street or in a lot?

8. Must I be a member of the VHS to use the library, or is there a nonmember fee for use? What is that fee?

9. Do you have any pamphlets that could be mailed to me in advance addressing any of these questions?

10. Are there times that are busier than others in the library? Which would be the best days to visit for research purposes?

Thank you for your assistance, I am enclosing a self-addressed stamped envelope for your reply. I look forward to visiting you in December.

Sincerely,

Marie B. Smith
10 Genealogy Drive
Anytown, USA
999-555-1111
mbsmith@aaa.com

Enclosure: SASE

Sample Letter to Request Information About a Facility

better prepared to research when you get there. Always ask the clerk, by letter or phone, what is the *best* time to come. Many have certain busy days when they would not be available to assist you. I have had town clerks tell me what day is voter registration and the opening of hunting season, thereby sparing me the frustration of trying to utilize a busy office, and an overtaxed staff, for my research. You will, most times, get a much better reception and be perceived as considerate when you do this. I have found that it opens doors when you are aware and courteous of the time constraints of the person who will be assisting you. Make an appointment if possible, and let the person know which records interest you. If they are stored elsewhere, either within the building or not, it gives the staff time to retrieve them for your visit. I have actually had clerks look up the names in the index and place markers in the volumes to indicate records I may be interested in. Treat the staff as you would like to be treated. (See chapters six, seven, and nine for additional information.)

Things you should ask about any facility you will be visiting:

- What are the regular research hours?
- Will there be any scheduled closures (for example, for inventory, asbestos removal) of the facility during the period you wish to visit?
- Are there any restrictions pertaining to the use of the records?
- Can briefcases, notebooks, and laptop computers be taken into the research room or must they be put in a locker?
- Can the records be photocopied and what is the cost? Is the copying self-serve or done only by a staff member?
- Are there any lunch or coffee break facilities that are open to researchers? Are there vending machines for your use?
- What type of parking is available: on the street, metered, or in a parking lot?
- Is there public transportation to and from the facility?
- Are there any other facilities in the immediate neighborhood that may be of interest to you?

Important

Some of these questions may seem unnecessary, but every one has been added to the list due to surprises I or others have encountered during our research. The question regarding closures was one of my costly lessons a few years ago. I had called a state historical society to get hours for my research trip. The clerk gladly gave me their regular operating hours but neglected to inform me that they would be closing for six months starting on October first of that year. I drove three-and-a-half hours only to find the facility closed and a sign on the door indicating they were closed for asbestos removal. That's a lesson I do not care to repeat!

When you are traveling a great distance, perhaps to visit relatives, writing ahead can also be a tool to get into a facility that would normally not be open on the day you will be there. One society that I wanted to visit was only open on Friday afternoons from 1 to 4 P.M. By writing ahead and telling them I was going to be in the area on Monday and Tuesday only, they offered to open the

Tip

facility by appointment just for me. What a wonderful surprise that was! I ended up joining their historical society and have become friends with several members who now inform me whenever new information on my ancestors is received. You never know what will happen until you try.

GENEALOGY BOOKSELLERS

Another way you can have the post office working for you is to get your name on several mailing lists for genealogical book publishers and suppliers. Most have toll-free numbers and will send you periodical catalogs listing the wonderful new books that are available. It is the best kind of junk mail I receive. I love to sit down with a cup of coffee and read the catalog from cover to cover. If you do not have a good genealogical bookstore nearby, it may be the only means you have to learn about the new materials on the market. Most of the genealogical publishers and suppliers also have Web sites, and orders can be placed directly over the Internet or by phone using a credit card.

Another type of item that you can have come to you is one of the many genealogical publications currently on the market. Most of the genealogical magazines are only obtainable by mail. Check your library for one of the many publications and look at several issues to see what is being offered. Most are published either bimonthly or quarterly and will be delivered right to your door! Advertisements in such magazines are always geared toward the genealogical and historical researcher. The articles are informative and provide many learning experiences for the researcher. This is especially true if you do not have an active genealogical society to network with others or the opportunity to attend genealogical conferences on a regular basis.

GENEALOGICAL SOCIETIES

There are many nationwide, statewide, and countywide organizations that you can join. Most have a regular newsletter with educational articles and upcoming events. Societies, such as the National Genealogical Society (NGS), Federation of Genealogical Societies (FGS), and the New England Historic Genealogical Society (NEHGS) offer educational conferences in different parts of the United States. Becoming a member of one of these organizations will keep you posted on what is happening in the genealogical world beyond your doorstep.

The New England Historic Genealogical Society (NEHGS) in Boston, Massachusetts, has a circulating library for members to use. **This service allows you to borrow books via the mail that may not be available in your area.** Currently they have more than fifteen thousand books that can be borrowed by members for a nominal shipping fee, and they will be shipped directly to you! NEHGS also has a sales catalog, making many genealogical books available for purchase that you may not be able to obtain otherwise.

Library/Archive Source

Sources

TOLL-FREE NUMBERS AND INTERNET ADDRESSES FOR BOOK AND SUPPLY CATALOGS

1. Betterway Books (F&W Publications), (800) 289-0963, <www.familytreemagazine.com/store>

2. Everton Publishers (genealogical forms and publications), (800) 443-6325, <www.everton.com>

3. Genealogical Publishing Company, (800) 296-6687, <www.genealogybookshop.com>

4. Heritage Books, (800) 393-7709, <www.heritagebooks.com>

5. Picton Press, (800) 742-8667, <www.pictonpress.com>

6. Ancestry, Inc. (genealogical charts and publications), (800) 531-1790, <www.ancestry.com>

7. Genealogy Unlimited (also sells forms and maps), (800) 666-4363, <www.itsnet.com/home/genun/publis_html/index.html>

8. Appleton's Books & Genealogy (also sells genealogical software), (800) 777-3601, <www.appletons.com/genealogy>

9. Gaylord Brothers (archival storage supplies), (800) 448-6160, <www.gaylord.com>

10. Hearthstone Books (genealogical books and supplies), (888) 960-3300, <www.hearthstonebooks.com>

11. Jonathan Sheppard Books, <http://www.jonathansheppardbooks.com>

12. National Genealogical Society, (800) 473-0060, E-mail <bookstore@ngsgenealogy.org>

Another wonderful source for borrowing books is the National Genealogical Society, which also has a lending library. Many of their nearly thirty thousand volumes are available to members by mail for a nominal fee, and an online catalog is available at <http://www.ngsgenealogy.org/library>. By visiting the many library sites and catalogs online, you can determine what books are available, either at the facility, by interlibrary loan, or through the mail.

MICROFILM RENTAL PROGRAMS

One company called Heritage Quest (formerly AGLL—American Genealogical Lending Library) and one government agency, the National Archives Record Administration (NARA), also rent rolls of microfilm to the researcher. **If you have no local access to the census records, ship passenger lists,**

Microfilm Source

revolutionary pension records, and so on, you may be able to borrow them by mail from Heritage Quest or NARA and use them at a local facility with a microfilm reader. Most libraries have microfilm and microfiche readers, since many newspapers and other publications are in microform. The cost for rental from HQ or NARA is minimal, and some films can also be purchased directly from Heritage Quest. If you have a Family History Center nearby, you can rent thousands of films directly from the main library in Salt Lake City for use in the local center. Again, the cost is minimal and the number of available records is staggering. Both the Family History Center and Heritage Quest have catalogs. Heritage Quest also has a printed catalog. (See their Web site at <www.heritagequest.com> for information.) The Family History Library offers a catalog on CD-ROM at the local facility, and online at <www.familysearch.org>. Information about the National Archives microfilm rental program is also available at <http://www.nara.gov/publications/microfilm/micrent.html>.

Another service you can utilize is borrowing books through the public library's interlibrary loan program. Check with your library for availability and access to this service. If your library offers the service, you can borrow books from other libraries for your use at your hometown library.

These are just some of the many services that can bring information to you. There are more and more such services being offered through genealogical societies and organizations throughout the United States. By using a few minutes of time at home, you can have an almost endless supply of information coming right to you!

In the next chapter, we will venture into the wonderful world of the computer and the Internet.

FOUR

Getting Your Computer and the Internet to Work for You

With the explosion of the Internet and genealogical resources available online, much of your indexing and preliminary research can be done without leaving home! Use the information cautiously, as it is only as accurate as the source. Just because it comes off the computer doesn't make it correct! As with any other type of record, transcriptions contain errors. You are relying on another person's interpretation of the original record. All indexes contain errors to different degrees. Understanding these databases can make the difference between success and failure.

One of the most useful benefits the Internet provides is the "networking" with other researchers. **With the USGenWeb (<http://www.USGenWeb.com>) and RootsWeb (<http://www.RootsWeb.com>) sites, you can correspond electronically with others researching the same surname or region of a state or country.** There are Web sites for every county in the United States with an amazing amount of information in electronic format just waiting for you. I have even obtained official copies of vital record documents from Italy via an online request. It's truly amazing what can be accomplished with a computer and the "genealogy bug" working in tandem.

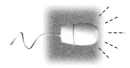

Internet Source

THE USGENWEB

The original goal of the USGenWeb project, at <http://www.USGenWeb.com> was to establish a Web site for every county in the United States, staffed strictly by volunteers. This goal has been met, and there is now a push to establish Web sites for all foreign jurisdictions. These county Web pages vary greatly depending on the volunteers, what records are available, and how often the page is updated. This is a wonderful undertaking and the volunteer effort is tremendous. Many of these counties also maintain mailing lists you can subscribe to. Mailing lists are formed by a group of people with a common interest, such as a surname, locality, or ethnic group. Some offer the list in mail mode or digest mode.

Mail mode simply means that all messages posted to the list in a given day are forwarded to you as individual E-mails. It is as simple as clicking on "reply" to respond to a posting when they are received in mail mode.

With digest mode, the messages are grouped together as one large E-mail and sent together, usually daily. I highly recommend the digest mode if it is offered. It is much simpler to keep the messages contained in just one E-mail rather than in many individual messages. The only problem I have encountered is when you wish to reply to one of the postings. If you simply click on the reply button, you will be sending the entire message back, and it will show up again in tomorrow's posting. I find it much better to select and then copy the sender's E-mail address and paste it into a new message. If you want to send the message to the list as well, you will need to do the same with that E-mail address. It is a little less convenient when responding to the specific message, but it far outweighs having twenty or more separate messages sent to your mailbox every day.

Most E-mail programs will allow you to set up individual folders for E-mails already received. I have set up a folder for each of the mailing lists I subscribe to. After I read and respond to the messages, I move the entire message to the appropriate folder. This way I can go back at a later date and review the messages again should I find new information regarding my search, and I'm not dealing with hundreds of messages in my inbox. Since the folders are titled with the county name or surname of the mailing list, I know which folder to look in for a particular subject.

Printed Source

There are many books available on the subject of E-mail and mailing lists. **Books on genealogy and the use of computers can offer more valuable tips when using this technology.** *The Genealogy Forum on America Online*, by George G. Morgan, is one such book. It deals with many subjects that America Online offers its customers. It includes a chapter titled, "Introduction to Genealogy and the Online Environment," which offers tips and information about primary and secondary sources, how to document information found in cyberspace, and citing your electronic sources properly.

Another helpful book is *Genealogy Online for Dummies,* by Matthew L. Helm and April Leigh Helm. I constantly use this book and have learned many tricks of the trade from the suggestions provided. The authors cover the basics of genealogical research as well as the use of the Internet for information. Lists of genealogical publications available on the Web, sites for beginners, and information about the computer world as well as chapters on designing Web pages cover most topics you will need to get started.

Books providing electronic addresses to obtain a myriad of genealogical records are also prevalent in bookstores. *The Internet for Dummies* by John Levine, Margaret Levine Young, and Carol Baroudi is a helpful book for the Internet and genealogical research. Check your local booksellers to see what is available and then choose the one that seems most helpful to your research. Many of these books are available in the reference, genealogical, or computer sections of libraries and stores, as well as with Internet booksellers.

Many of the USGenWeb county pages have volunteers who offer free searches in specified books. This can be a real time-saver for many genealogical researchers. Just being able to have someone look up a name or subject in one book can save you time looking for that specific book. Since many of these volunteers list the books in which they will do searches, you may learn about a book that you didn't know existed. There are so many benefits to the mailing lists, and it is just one more way you can have information come to you.

Another aspect I have found useful on the USGenWeb state and county sites are the links to towns within a given county. On these more localized Web pages, I have found cemetery listings, death records, local directories, and census transcriptions, just to name a few. Most contain the list of volunteers willing to do the searches and researchers you can hire. They also contain information on local repositories that may not appear in the large published books mentioned in the previous chapters.

RootsWeb

The RootsWeb site, at <http://www.RootsWeb.com>, is along the same lines as the USGenWeb, except that all of the mailing lists and home pages are divided by surname rather than locality. I subscribe to several surname mailing lists, especially for those particularly stubborn ancestral names. Information is constantly being E-mailed back and forth among researchers interested in that particular surname. Most sites allow you to post a query regarding someone with that surname and the responses are quite varied but helpful. I have had several major breakthroughs thanks to the surname mailing lists. Locating distant relatives is also a plus that frequently occurs.

States, counties, and ethnic genealogical sites offer an abundance of information as well as instructional articles, indexes, and information regarding research facilities, and local volunteers. **There is even a Web site called "Genealogical Acts of Kindness," at <http://raogk.rootsweb.com/index.html>, where people grant favors (free searches, copies, etc.) to other researchers, hoping that the favor will be passed on to another researcher.** You can also visit the "Genealogy's Most Wanted" site at <http://www.citynet.net/mostwanted/index.html> and post a query regarding your most difficult ancestors.

Many people who post on the state or county lists actually live there and offer to do searches in certain publications and books. I have done free searches for people at the local National Archives branch in exchange for information from their area. Bartering is a great way to obtain information while using your time efficiently. Our ancestors bartered their services, so why shouldn't we? I go to a National Archives facility almost every week, so to give an hour to look up something is time wisely spent, especially in exchange for research that would be difficult for me to do myself.

Definitions

Query—A brief request for information usually placed in a publication or on the Internet.

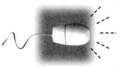

Internet Source

E-NEWSLETTERS AND HOW-TO ARTICLES

There are many wonderful E-newsletters posted on the Internet. Some are updated daily or weekly, while others are updated monthly. An E-newsletter is simply a newsletter that is distributed via E-mail rather than postal mail. By posting newsletters online, an organization can reach many more potential members than by the traditional mailing route and at far less expense. Many of us would never know that certain groups existed if they did not post the E-newsletters.

Several useful E-newsletters available through the Ancestry.com site are
- Dick Eastman's "Online Genealogy Newsletter"
- George G. Morgan's "Along Those Lines"
- Myra Vanderpool Gormley's "Shaking Your Family Tree"
- Dear Myrtle's "Genealogy Column"

The Ancestry.com home page, <http://www.Ancestry.com>, also offers how-to articles and access to archived back issues of these newsletters.

Ancestry.com also offers a "Learning Center," which contains information to make family history research easier. Topics include help for beginners; guides to genealogical records; reference section; computer genealogy and other research; and maps, gazetteers and other geographical tools.

The Genealogy.com and FamilyTreeMaker.com Web sites also present how-to articles and helpful tips on many types of research. You will want to visit these sites on a regular basis and read the articles. The authors of the newsletters and articles are among the top genealogists in the country, and you can reap the rewards of their expertise presented there. Genealogy .com has an online university that contains wonderful information for all levels of researchers.

Several genealogical publications maintain Web sites and lists of articles that have appeared in previous and current issues. Two such publications are *Family Tree Magazine* (<http://www.familytreemagazine.com>) and *Family Chronicle Magazine* (<http://www.familychronicle.com>). **The *Family Tree Magazine* site has a "SuperSearch" feature that searches hundreds of genealogical sites for you.** The site offers free weekly research tips and leads on new resources by E-mail subscription, a bookstore with genealogical books available for purchase, free forms to download from its site, and other notable features worth looking at.

Timesaver

The *RootsWeb Review* is published once each week and lists all of the new surname mailing lists available to the researcher. The articles contained in the E-newsletter are wonderful and offer many tips and information as well as educational information. The *RootsWeb Review* is sent to over 350,000 E-mail addresses every week. That is a sizeable number of people subscribing to just one newsletter.

Using the educational and informative sites dedicated to genealogical research can provide you with an almost endless list of research possibilities. The Internet is available to you whether you have fifteen minutes or more any time of the day or night. You can accomplish an amazing amount of research and networking using the E-newsletters, instructional articles, and mailing lists available to you.

RESEARCH SITES

Another great tool on the Internet is the many sites that offer indexes to several types of records. **There are a number of large genealogical sites that offer online databases and indexes to records.** They are

- Ancestry.com <http://www.Ancestry.com>
- Genealogy.com <http://www.Genealogy.com>
- FamilySearch <http://www.FamilySearch.org>
- FamilyTreeMaker.com <http://www.FamilyTreeMaker.com>

Sources

Some of these databases are free, while others are by subscription only. When you think of your time as money, the subscription fee is reasonable and usually a bargain at that. Check out the offerings, talk to other researchers who use these services, and decide which are worth your money and which are not. Most sites provide free lists of their holdings. There is no perfect site for all researchers. Like your filing system, it must address your needs to be useful and worthwhile.

Ancestry.com adds a new database every weekday. The databases are free for the first ten days after posting and then become accessible by subscription only. They offer a daily E-newsletter that is automatically sent to your E-mail address. Every weekday, without having to do anything, I get their newsletter filled with information regarding new books, how-to articles, tips, updates on facilities, and news releases that would be hard, if not impossible, to obtain with my time restraints. The newsletter contains articles of an educational nature that can help you learn about specific record types, and it offers information regarding other Web sites that pertain to that particular subject. I find it very helpful to learn about a record type, gain information about the research, and get Web site addresses all in one article. This is also a great way to keep up with the new databases that are added daily, which can help you access these databases for free or keep you current on all the offerings. Ancestry.com has a daily "Ancestry Quick Tip" feature that has provided me with new research possibilities. I am amazed at how many of the posted tips were things that I had never thought of. Learning from other researchers' experience can save you many hours of frustration.

Ancestry.com features a "Family History Favorites" award every week. This goes to a Web site that provides valuable information or services to the genealogical and educational community as a whole. Many of the sites have proved to be helpful to me, and I probably would not have discovered them on my own, at least not in this lifetime!

FamilyTreeMaker.com offers indexes to the many Family Tree Maker CDs that can either be purchased or used at your genealogical library. If you have ever used any of these indexes, you know that it is much easier to search one database (containing all Family Tree Maker CDs) than each CD individually. This also allows you to prepare at home a list of the CDs you will need to look at the next time you go to the library. Preparation is the key!

Another site that provides new avenues of research is CyndisList.com (<http://www.CyndisList.com>). This site has more than 60,000 links to other sites of genealogical interest. The sites are divided by country, state, ethnic groups, and subjects to make finding what you are looking for much easier. The sheer number of these specialty sites is amazing. You would have to spend a great deal of time to find these sites on your own or use search engines. Cyndi Howells has done the work for you and developed a gold mine for genealogical researchers in the process. I visit her site regularly to see what new sites have been added to her amazing compilation. Howells also has several helpful books about genealogical research on the Internet.

There are many books on the market (see the bibliography) that can assist you in using the Internet to its best advantage. You can contact state record office sites and then print the blank forms required for a written inquiry. The information found at these sites often includes not only the forms, but also information regarding what records they have available, the cost to obtain them, and any restrictions to accessing them. This saves you the time of writing to get this information and having your request returned to you or ignored because you failed to include something or to meet certain requirements. Again, time is money!

THE PROS AND CONS OF CD-ROMS
(and Online Indexes)

Important

Online databases can save you many hours of research if you use them wisely. You must first understand how the database is created and how to maximize your search results. This takes some practice. **Most online or CD-ROM indexes or databases are created through either data entry, scanning the document as an image, or by optical character recognition (OCR) software.**

Data entry is just what the name implies. A person "keys" the information, or data, into a computerized file, which can then be searched. Depending on the program that searches the database, you may have the ability to search every word or by fields of information. Keep in mind that every time any piece of information is transcribed, whether the original is handwritten or typed, errors can and do occur. The database is only as good as the data-entry person who made it.

Scanned databases are image-based. That means that the image on the screen is a picture, and as far as the computer knows, there are no words on the screen, only a "picture" or image. Many books are scanned this way, making the index for the database only as good as the book index. Just because it is on the CD or computer doesn't necessarily make the index any more complete than the original.

Databases that have been created using OCR are scanned images that the

Tip

TIPS THAT YIELD RESULTS WHEN SURFING THE WEB

1. Search for sites by location.
2. Search for sites by surname.
3. Search by ethnic origins.
4. Search by subject.
5. Search by record types.
6. Search by time frame or era.
7. Search by occupation or military service.
8. Visit already existing genealogical sites to see what links are available.

computer then "translates" into text. Accuracy in the translation is dependent upon the typeface style, size, and readability. Errors can and do occur. This type of scanning requires a person to reread the translation to correct any misread letters or words. The database is basically the same as a data-entered one and is text-based and usually completely searchable. OCR can be a difficult process when you consider the various typestyles in use over the last two centuries. If more than one typestyle or font is used within the publication, it becomes even more complicated to scan, read, and translate.

Most CDs and databases provide instructions regarding the best way to search the information included on the CD or Web site. Be sure to read the instructions to get the most out of the database. The phrase, "penny wise and pound foolish" applies here. **Saving a few minutes by not reading the instructions will cost you far more time later.** Many programs will provide certain techniques to get the best results. This may or may not include the use of "wild cards" in the search process. Wild cards are useful when you are searching for a name that is misspelled. Instead of typing Woodborough, you could type Woodbo* and the program will search for anything that begins with Woodbo regardless of what the remainder of the word is. This solves the problem of the Woodboro or Woodborow spelling.

Warning

Some databases and CDs also allow you to search using the Soundex coding system that is used for some U.S. federal census indexes. Soundex translates a name into a letter and three-digit code based on the way the name sounds, not by the literal spelling. This can be especially useful with immigrant and commonly misspelled names. Not all of the possible spellings will code the same, so it is important to code several different spellings to see if they are the same.

To Soundex a name, you must first write it out the way it is most commonly spelled.

Step By Step

Example: McDonald

First, write down the first letter of the surname (M). Now cross off the vowels as well as the W, H, and Y consonants. These consonants are disregarded because W and H are often silent when the names are pronounced. The Y is disregarded because it often acts as a vowel. If, however, the first letter of the surname is a vowel or one of these three consonants, you still use it just like you do the letter M.

You now have: McD~~ONA~~LD   M __ __ __

Take the remaining letters (CDNLD) and code only three of the remaining letters using this chart:

THE NUMBER:	REPRESENTS THE LETTERS:
1	B P F V
2	C S K G J Q X Z
3	D T
4	L
5	M N
6	R

Disregard the letters A, E, I, O, U, W, H, and Y.

The first letter is a C and will code as a 2.
The second letter is a D and codes as a 3.
The third letter is an N and codes as a 5.

This gives you the code M235. Since the code only consists of a letter and three numbers, disregard the remaining letters. M235 is one Soundex code for the name McDonald. Try spelling the name several different ways, like the census takers did, and see what code results you come up with. Most of the time it will remain the same, although occasionally it will differ. The spelling MacDonell would also code as M235 since the A is disregarded when you cross out the vowels. If the name has been spelled McDonnald, you must apply the one exception to the Soundex rule (isn't there always at least one?) If two or more consonants appear side by side that would be coded the same (for example SS, SCK, CK, CZ), disregard all but the first occurrence, including the first letter of the name. (For example, with the surname Schmidt, disregard the C since it is the same code as the first letter of the name. The proper code would then be S530.) For the misspelled McDonnald surname, you would then have a code of M235, the same code as before. If you do not have enough letters remaining to get three digits, fill the spaces with the digit 0. You should always have a code consisting of a letter and three digits. Names that begin with a prefix (Mc, Van, Di, O, St., etc.) should be coded with and without the prefix. The surname McDonald coded without the prefix results in a code of D543.

Most databases and CDs that allow for a Soundex search do not require that you know the code. The computer will do that for you automatically. However, you will need to complete a search using each spelling variation to be sure that the search was a complete one. I try manually spelling and coding the name several ways to see if the codes change before I choose the "Soundex search" option while using a database. Only then can you be assured that you have done a complete search of the file.

Keep in mind that the computer is a very literal machine. It will do what you tell it to do, not what you want it to do. If you ask it to find Hale, it will not know that it might also be spelled Hail. Few searches are done by the sound of the name like the Soundex searches, but rather by the literal spelling. Interestingly, Hale, Hail, Hayl would all code the same (H400) under the Soundex system since the only codeable letter following the H is the L. Knowing this will make your search more fruitful. You must do a separate search of every spelling variation you can think of or have encountered if the Soundex option is not offered. If there is a typographical error in the data entry, you may never find the entry. Don't be discouraged. Indexes, whether electronic or in printed form, are notoriously incomplete. Just because the person you are looking for doesn't appear in the index does not mean she isn't in the record.

Warning

Many indexing errors occur because the indexer is reading old, faded documents, is interpreting someone else's handwriting, or may be unfamiliar with an unusual name. The problems that exist for the indexer are the same ones you will encounter when looking at handwritten documents. There is an interesting book, *A Practical Guide to the "Misteaks" Made in Census Indexes*, edited by Richard Saldana (see the bibliography). It provides you with insight into the errors that can and do creep into any index, whether electronic or printed.

When dealing with online indexes, there may be no instructions or hints to improve your searches. If that is the case, you will have to spend a little time with the specific index to see exactly how it operates. Some indexes, both online and on CD, will provide you with a screen showing only the exact matches. Others will take you to a list, showing the closest match to your search. You can then scroll up or down to view the list just as you would in a book index. I prefer the second type of search because it gives me the opportunity to look at all of the names within a certain range, many times producing the name I was actually looking for. If you are not sure what first or middle name your subject used (they love to confuse us), you can simply request the surname and scroll down through all of the people included in the index under that surname.

A problem that has always existed with any type of index is omissions. How do you know if that database even includes the town or county in question? When looking for an ancestor in Rutland County, Vermont, in the 1850 census, I first went to the printed index. After trying every possible spelling of the name, I incorrectly concluded that he was not residing in Vermont in 1850. A subsequent search of the specific town revealed that he was there all along. I then checked several other residents of the county with the index book and realized that most, if not all, of Rutland County had been omitted from the index. That taught me a lesson that I have always applied to online

Tip

or CD indexes I encounter: Never assume the index is complete.

When using any online or CD index, it is helpful to start a search with as many specifics as I know.

Case Study

Example: When searching the online AIS (Accelerated Indexing System) Census Indexes (available on <Ancestry.com>), I begin by entering the information as I know it, such as James L. Douglas, Blair County, Pennsylvania, and perhaps the year 1860. If I get no matching entries, I try spelling the last name as Douglass, as I have frequently seen it recorded in this manner, and I try a Soundex search. If I still get no matching entries, I eliminate the middle initial, and then the first name, and try the search again. You never know if James may have been indexed as Jim, or by a middle name, or just an initial. If that still produces no results, I eliminate the name altogether. This has helped me many times to determine if the county in question is even included in the index. If Blair County, Pennsylvania, in 1860 produces no hits, then the whole county is probably not included in the database. I now know that I will have to consult a book index or look through the entire county in the 1860 census to find him. Just because he does not appear in the index doesn't mean he was not there. There are countless omissions in any index and many indexes are terribly incomplete.

I also try the search using the different names, but deleting the county name and leaving just the state just in case James migrated into another county. By doing a thorough search and using *all fields* as clues, you will get a better picture of the database in question. Understanding the drawbacks to any index will make you a more creative searcher. How many ways can you spell Smith?

Research Tip

Another trick to finding people in the online indexes for censuses, is to enter another surname that you know appears in the same county and town. When you find someone in the resulting entries, note the town, county, and page number indicated. Then go back to the search screen and put in the town, county, state, and page number. You will get a list of all of the people (mostly just the heads of the households) on that page in the census. Now continue by entering each subsequent page number before and after the first one you tried. You can look at a whole town this way. With this trick, I have found the person I wanted, usually spelled some horrific way that I never would have tried. I have also found people that I didn't even know were there.

There have been occasions where the town did not seem to be in the index. Upon further searching, I discovered that the town name had been misspelled. Starksboro was spelled St. Arksboro by the indexer. When I entered the town name under that spelling (and I tried every possible way to enter it), I still got "No matching entries" for a reply. I then entered the county and page number and found the entries for Starksboro. Be creative and persistent! Spending a few minutes playing with a database may yield positive results well worth the extra time spent, especially when it can be done at home, at any hour of the day or night, and at your own pace.

Once I have located the person in question, I print out the page listing the specifics of the find. This gives me the information I need to look up the actual census, and I write my notes right on the printed page. I always know to whom the notes pertain. If there are five men named James Douglas in Blair County, I will need to look at all of them. A quick look can often eliminate most, if not all, of the incorrect ones. Since I know his wife's name and his approximate age, I can look for these pieces of information to single out my family. The others I mark as "incorrect family" and file it with my research logs for that family. This documents that I looked at all of the James Douglases in question.

Another aspect to watch in online indexes is whether or not middle initials affect the search. The Social Security Death Index (available as a free database on Ancestry.com), for example, disregards the middle initial although it may appear on the record. Some indexes allow the middle initial to affect the search, while others do not. Try out a few names to find out how the database handles such information. Many of the indexes will allow you to enter "J. Douglas" as criteria for the search. They will then produce all of the individuals bearing the surname Douglas whose first name begins with J, while others will only consider J. Douglas individuals as matches. For this reason, I usually try using only the surname and then look at the matching individuals. I have located many people using this method that I would probably not have found doing a traditional search due to misspelled given names, or the use of middle or nicknames in the index.

Warning

The only database that searches the name by its sound rather than literal spelling is on the FamilySearch Web site managed by the Church of Jesus Christ of Latter-day Saints (Mormons). This database groups like-sounding names together. You will find Cline, Klein, and Kline grouped together. With a Soundex search, the first letter would change the code, thereby requiring two or more searches. Kline would be K450, while Cline would be C450. You should still check to see if any of your spellings might be grouped separately. (Spelling can really confuse the search at times.) This is a great way to see how many creative ways the surname has been spelled. It might surprise you to find an additional spelling or two that you had not considered.

Example: I was researching the name Waite in the census indexes. I tried every way I could think of to misspell the name. The spelling of Wait, Whaite, Waite, and Wate all came to mind. But I had not considered one that turned out to be golden: Weight, which was the spelling in the index. You would think that someone phonetically spelling the name would not use the more complicated and rather unusual spelling of a fairly easy name. Another family name, spelled Fopiano was misspelled Phopiano. Again, be creative and persistent, and check every possibility.

Case Study

As long as you understand the good, the bad, and the ugly of online and CD databases, they can provide you with many leads to further your research. The best part is that the Internet never closes. As many of us have discovered, 2 A.M. seems to sneak up on us at times. You can really get lost on the technology superhighway!

EVALUATING AND CITING THE SOURCES FROM CDs AND ONLINE INFORMATION

Important

Citing Sources

Another important point that has to be made is evaluating and citing your sources when using the Internet or CD-ROMs for information. This can become a problem in itself. **The proper citation is not just the CD number and publisher, but the document the information came from.** Many CDs contain information gleaned from several books that are combined on one disk without indicating which information came from which book or publication. Some, but not all, CDs explain which of the several books included on the disk contained the specific information. Many CDs only provide the information and a list of the books that were included, leaving you to figure out which one contained that specific piece of information. Again, check the instructions contained on the CDs or the information provided on the Web site regarding what was included in the database. Cryptic citations are not unusual, just as in books. You must understand the abbreviations contained in any information regardless of its source. Look in the preface of the book or the instructions for the CD for a clear explanation of these abbreviations or citations. Be a smart consumer! Ask questions of any database or index you use. Make sure you understand everything you are reading.

Two valuable books for learning and understanding proper citation and analysis of your sources are *Evidence! Citation and Analysis for the Family Historian,* by Elizabeth Shown Mills, and *Cite Your Sources,* by Richard Lackey. Several excellent articles have also appeared in online newsletters. Understanding how to properly cite your sources, whether from published or electronic media, is crucial to the success of your research. Knowing how to successfully analyze the reliability of those sources can save you hours of research time. Just because you found it in a book or on a computer does not make the information correct!

If the CD or database in question does not indicate which source contained that specific piece of information, you should (yes, you really should) look at every item that is contained within the database. These will usually be listed in the introduction to the database. Record the listings and check them all, one by one, until you find the correct source. I guarantee that you will be *at least* two to three generations away from the original source. Most compilations in electronic media are taken from published books. Those books were also compilations of either the original records or another publication. Have I made my point clear?

Many online databases will list the source of the information, such as AIS Census Indexes. Once you look at the actual census record, use the census citation to document your record. Use the online databases as an *index* to the original source, not as your actual source. By actually looking at the original source, you will be sure that the index is correct and contains no errors. You will be surprised to see how many errors creep into all indexes.

Don't get me wrong. Electronic indexes will save you a lot of time in your research as long as you understand their pros and cons and have a realistic expectation of the results. Using them whenever you have an opportunity can lead you to many other records as well. Some weekends I spend most of a day online (in between loading the washer, dryer, and dishwasher) trying the different databases, search engines, and genealogical sites available. The hardest part seems to be keeping my husband and daughters from "stealing" the computer when I abandon the keyboard for housework!

ONLINE LIBRARY CATALOGS

Another important online tool is library catalogs. Many libraries are now making their catalogs available to Internet users. This can help you find that rare book that has your family mentioned in it, or contains the history of a particular county but is either no longer in print or not available in your area. Many such books and publications fit that category. Many town and county histories for the United States were printed in limited quantity and, therefore, are difficult to find. Many are now being duplicated in electronic format for inclusion on CDs or online databases. As the copyright expires on a book and it comes into public domain, it can be duplicated in electronic format.

Use the online catalogs to help plan your next research trip to the facility or area. **By knowing what the facility holds and what unique collections it may have, you can plan your research trip more thoroughly.** Again, do as much of your work at home *before* you go to ensure efficient use of your time once you get there.

Timesaver

Check the catalogs for manuscript collections, too. These materials are usually unique to the facility and are worth spending time researching. Unlike manuscripts, many books can be obtained through your library or interlibrary loan. Don't waste your research time using materials available locally. Use the unique records, such as manuscripts and newspapers.

FINDING LOCAL HISTORY SOURCES

Another great research tool for the Internet user is the regional Web pages that contain information regarding the state, county, or town of interest to you. All states in the United States have a Web page thanks to the USGenWeb project, which I mentioned earlier in this chapter. The original goal of the project was to have a volunteer-manned Web page for every county in the United States. They have achieved this goal and are now reaching out to encompass other countries as well.

By going to USGenWeb.com, you can navigate to the state of your choice using several different methods. If you are good at geography, you can click on the graphic map of the United States. If, like most people, you cannot identify the states by their shape, they have provided a chart to select from. Or you can also click on a simple text list. Depending on the speed of your Internet connection, the text list may be the fastest.

Once you are connected to the state, there are breakdowns to the counties, and then, in some cases, to actual towns within the county and specific record groups. The quality and amount of information provided on each individual site varies a great deal. Some sites are monitored and updated more often than others. All in all, they are a great resource for the genealogical and historical researcher, especially those of us with limited research time. We should be very grateful for the hard work done by these volunteers.

I have found many cemetery transcriptions, vital records, family information, and county histories, on these sites. I have even printed out pictures of my ancestor's gravestones that were submitted by a volunteer. There is usually an E-mail connection to the Webmaster, or the ability to post a query to the site. Many of the sites archive the past queries, and these can also be searched. You will then find out if anyone else is researching the same surnames as you.

By subscribing to the mailing list for a specific subject or name, you will be sent all of the messages posted to the list. This can get overwhelming at times, but you can have your name removed from the mailing at any time. If given a choice, I usually sign up for the digest mode of the list. By selecting the digest mode, you will receive just one E-mail containing all the messages posted that day, along with a table of contents of the posts. Lists that do not have a digest mode will send every E-mail that was posted as an individual E-mail. One list I subscribed to had more than fifty postings in the first twenty-four hours after I subscribed. Yikes! You will find that some lists tend to post everything, whether on the topic of the list or not, while others filter out extraneous messages. I use my delete button on a regular basis. I would rather make the decision as to whether the posting is of interest than take a chance on missing an important one. And the delete button is so easy to use!

Tip

When posting queries to lists, try to be as short and precise as possible. After reading the postings from several lists over a short period of time, you will discover what is and is not acceptable or desirable. Use the same guidelines as you would if you were requesting the information via the mail. Pay attention to grammar, spelling (Isn't spell-check wonderful?), brevity, clarity, and common courtesy when posting. Always remember that the person reading your inquiry has no previous knowledge of the subject. Many postings such as "I am researching John Smith in Massachusetts" have ended up in my recycling bin. Provide a time frame, precise location, or any information that will help the reader, and you will have a much better response rate. There is no "magic file" out there containing all of the information on your family and it is not all available online either.

Another technique that will help your messages stand out is to always list surnames in *all capital letters*. Once you get into the habit of recording them in this manner on your pedigree and family group sheets, you will find it easy to always type them this way as well. It is also nice to put the surnames at the beginning, again in all caps. When you get a large number of messages, it is easy to delete the ones you have no interest in simply by scanning the surnames and subject. If only everyone would follow this simple rule.

> Seeking parents/siblings of Hoxxey BARBER, b c1767 d 1837 in Rutland Co., VT, m to Rhoda RUSSELL 1790 in Mt. Holly, VT. Also researching ROGERS, HOLMES, ROUNDS families in VT.

As this example shows, being precise and definitive, and providing known names, dates, and locations gives the reader everything they need to recognize the individual. This is especially important with common names. Long, rambling messages can become tiresome to read and eat into your time very quickly. Don't succumb to the "E-mail monster." You don't want to waste your time reading every single posting to the list, or worse yet, responding to them. Pick and choose carefully. Remember that the Internet is still a place where most people are looking to get information rather than provide it.

Important

GENEALOGICAL PROGRAMS ABOUND!

The wide array of genealogical software programs on the market can be overwhelming to the uninitiated researcher. Determining which program is best for you can be time-consuming, but worth every minute. Many programs offer sample versions that are often available online, so you can try them before purchasing them. This is a good idea, especially since the complexity of entering data is the key ingredient to any genealogical software. All the fancy reports or charts mean nothing if you can't easily enter the data in the first place. **Any genealogical program should be in the GEDCOM format. GEDCOM stands for Genealogical Data Communication.** That's a fancy word that means the program can "talk to" or transfer its data to most other GEDCOM-formatted programs. This is especially important to the genealogist who doesn't want to reenter everything whenever he gets a new program or upgrades the current one. I think we all fit into that category. Another reason to make sure the program has a GEDCOM format is so you can easily share your entire database with other genealogists who also have GEDCOM-based programs.

\di'fin\ *vb*

Definitions

Many programs are available in office supply, computer, and specialty stores, but these packages are not necessarily the best. There are many excellent genealogical software programs that are not sold in these stores. Most genealogical book catalogs will offer genealogical and organizational programs as well. Talk to other genealogists to see what they use. Ask them what they like and don't like about their program. All of them have drawbacks. Which ones can you live with?

One important item was mentioned in chapter one: charts. As with any printed charts, the computer program should always print the standard six fields of information for every person on the pedigree or family group sheet. This should include birth date and place, marriage date and place, and death date and place. Some programs will print all six, while others will only print them if

See Also

you have information entered into that particular field. Several programs I have used over the years allow you to print the "empty fields" or not, depending on what you specify. This flexibility makes a good program even better.

The program should allow you to set the number of generations that will print on the pedigree chart. I find five or more generations on the same pedigree chart to be distracting. I prefer to print only four per page. But having the flexibility to print several different charts is ideal, especially when you want to condense your information to make it lighter to carry.

Along the same lines, the program should offer the option of printing or not printing your notes when you print the family group sheets. You should be able to customize your printouts. You should be given several options every time you instruct the program to print a report. Most will ask you what options or information you want to include and omit.

Another thing to look for is actually related to your printer. Many printers allow you to print double-sided pages. I stumbled across this quite by accident. My printer, a Hewlett Packard ink-jet printer, does not display it as a double-sided option, but rather calls it "book format." Play around a little with the print options to see what you can do. By printing my pedigree and family group sheets in book format, I carry half as much paper.

Reports are another feature to look for when purchasing a software package. Look at the list of reports that the program offers. Some offer the ability to customize a report to your needs. In the beginning, you may think that you won't really need to use this feature, but you will quickly outgrow a program that limits your report options. Handling databases is a major forte of computers. Why not use this power to your advantage? If you have to learn how to use the computer, make that learning time work for you.

Many types of reports will save you hours of research time later on. Once you have achieved the overwhelming task of entering all of that data into the program, the report features allow you to sort it in many different ways. Some programs allow you to print all of the events that happened in a specific locale or events that may be incorrect, or a list of the items that you have no data entered for. My program prints a "problems list" that includes such items as, "Mother was 120 years old when child was born." Oops! I typed in the wrong century. It's just a typographical error, but the program knows to question it. I run this report periodically to catch these mistakes. These are just a few of the many reports that can be generated. Think about the advantages of each type of report and how it can save you time, and you will see how learning to use it is worthwhile.

Some programs are designed for the professional genealogist and the person who is planning to publish the entered data. These programs sometimes have a very high learning curve and a higher purchase price. If you are not planning to publish and don't need a program with specialized features, why pay for the feature? **The *Genealogy Software Guide,* by Marthe Arends (see the bibliography), covers all of the aspects of genealogical database programs including a page listing what each contains, what restrictions there are, and so on that will give**

Printed Source

you a basis for comparison. It is not just a rundown of the programs offered, but rather a reference to what you should look for in a program, what equipment you need, Mac versus PC programs, and the list goes on. She provides many visual examples of the programs' input screens and printouts. Arends also provides lists of software vendors, Internet software resources, computer genealogy publications, and an appendix titled, "The Mystery of GEDCOM." Many program features listed in Arends's book pointed out items that I had not considered. The decision is yours and it must fit your needs, just like a filing system.

If you are just getting into computers, stick with a program that has a low learning curve and a fairly reasonable cost. As long as it is in GEDCOM format, you can always upgrade the program as you become more proficient. My two teenage daughters dragged me screaming and kicking into the twentieth century about ten years ago. I have since moved from a DOS-based system through Windows 3.1, Windows 95, and Windows 98. I remember thinking that I would never become proficient using the DOS program, but managed quite nicely—until my husband introduced me to Windows. I kept running upstairs to use the old DOS-based computer because I was comfortable with it and I knew how to get it to do what I wanted. Well, one day my husband decided to "remove" an integral part of the DOS computer and, thinking it was broken, I was forced to use his Windows-run machine. I have never gone back to the antiquated DOS machine. (I actually gave it away.)

We are always the most comfortable with what we know, but stretching our knowledge is rewarding. I actually advanced to the point that I created and maintained a Web site for almost a year. The moral of the story is that you can do it, although sometimes you have to be forced to!

Look for a program that is fairly easy to learn and to get started with, but has ample growth potential. Otherwise, you will be changing programs often and will have to relearn the basics every time you do. In the same light, stick with programs that have been around for a while. Have they gone through several upgrades? Do they print, either for purchase or through the software, an instruction manual? Has the program been reviewed in genealogical or computer publications? Is the program made to operate on your computer? Mac users have fewer programs to choose from than PC (IBM-based) users, but the Mac programs seem to be more fine-tuned and offer more features. Perhaps this is because feedback from Mac users is directed to only a couple of software companies, while IBM or PC companies have an abundance of programs and the feedback is more widely spread out.

For the most part, the software companies are open to genealogist's comments, but keep in mind that most programs are created by computer programmers, not genealogists. **For this reason, you as the consumer must be savvy to what you need the program to do. Will the program**
- accept a partial date, such as Nov 1754?
- allow for double dates (1723/4) to be entered?
- allow "before," "after," "between" when recording dates?

Reminder

Important

- allow you to specify how the surname is printed (all CAPS)?
- allow you to specify the date format (14 Nov 1724 vs. Nov. 14, 1724)?
- print your name and address on all forms?
- print the current date on all forms?
- allow you to print blank forms?
- restrict the number of people you can enter?
- restrict the number of characters or length of notes?
- restrict the number of notes you can add to an individual?
- allow for family notes as well as for individuals?
- allow you to rearrange the order of children in a given family?
- allow you unlimited events?
- allow you to create customized events?
- allow you to view your reports or forms before printing?
- allow for multiple parents listed?
- allow you to search the database by name or other criteria?
- allow you, and prompt you, to back up the database before exiting the program?
- point out mistakes or missing information?

Another feature to look for in a genealogy software program is the ability to print the information in several different formats. Most popular programs will print the entered information as pedigree or family group sheets, in book format (usually using the Register or National Genealogical Society Quarterly numbering systems, see pages 69 and 70), an alphabetical list, or a variety of other formats. Most programs will print reports of the descendants or ancestors of a person you specify in the database. This flexibility is an option that will become a necessity before too long, no matter how computer literate or illiterate you are today.

Talking to other computer users, subscribing to a computer users' mailing list, or attending computer user meetings will give you a good feel for which programs are most widely used and for what reasons. The most widely sold or available programs may not be the best, only the best marketed ones. There are several books that cover all, if not most, of the genealogical software programs on the market today (see the bibliography). A good, basic, easy-to-use program can usually be purchased for about fifty dollars. If a program is more expensive, be sure that you actually need the "bells and whistles" it offers. Remember that as long as it is GEDCOM compatible, you can always upgrade later when you are more proficient with the software. Most computer genealogists rarely stay with one program, but rather upgrade or change programs as their needs and abilities change. I actually have several programs on my computer. Until I find one program that has all the forms, reports, and features I need, I will continue to transfer the information between several different programs. I can then get the exact printout or feature I need. It's not as scary as it sounds, believe me. Once you have imported or exported a GEDCOM file, it will become old hat for you. Again, make the computer work for you. Utilize all of the features and save yourself time.

NUMBER SYSTEMS
Register System

The Register format was established by the New England Historic Genealogical Society for their quarterly journal, the *Register*. The numbering system begins with the earliest known ancestor, who is assigned the Arabic number 1 and proceeds in a descending format. The children of person number 1 are assigned Roman numerals in the order of their birth. When there is additional information on a child they are then designated with the next Arabic numeral such as 2 before their Roman numeral designation.

Example: 2. i. Hoxey^2 Barber Jr.

This indicates that his line is continued in section 2. Note that each generation carries a designation indicating the generation number in relationship to person 1 as well as the previous lineage in parenthesis after their name.

---

1.   Hoxxey^1 Barber was born ca 1767; married Rhoda Russell 12 Sep. 1790 in Mt. Holly, Rutland Co., Vermont; died 27 May 1837 at Mt. Holly.

Children; surname BARBER

2. i. Hoxey^2 Jr. b 06 Dec. 1791, d 05 Mar. 1864, m Nancy Emery

ii. Marabah^2, b 29 Feb. 1795 at Mt. Holly, Rutland Co., VT, m 18 Nov. 1818 at Mt. Holly to Isaac Dickerman, d 07 Nov. 1826 in Illinois.

3. iii. Rhoda^2, b 06 Dec. 1798, m 10 Dec. 1818 Lawson Earl, d 19 Dec. 1882.

2.   Hoxey^2 Barber Jr. (Hoxxey^1) was born 06 Dec. 1791 at Mt. Holly, VT, etc.

3.   Rhoda^2 Barber (Hoxxey^1) was born 06 Dec. 1798 at Mt. Holly, Rutland Co., Vermont; m Lawson Earl 10 Dec. 1818 at Mt. Holly, VT, died 19 Dec. 1882 at Mt. Holly, VT.

---

continued on page 70

NUMBER SYSTEMS—Continued
National Genealogical Society Quarterly System

National Genealogical Society Quarterly (NGSQ) or modified Register style is established in a similar manner, replacing the Roman numeral listing with Arabic numerals. A + sign is added before the person's number to indicate that the record continues elsewhere. Note that the generation numbers still appear following the names.

1.   Hoxxey[1] Barber was born ca 1767; married Rhoda Russell 12 Sep. 1790 in Mt. Holly, Rutland Co., Vermont; died 27 May 1837 at Mt. Holly.

      Children; surname BARBER

  + 2.   Hoxey[2] Jr. b 06 Dec. 1791, d 05 Mar. 1864, m Nancy Emery.

     3.   Marabah[2], b 29 Feb. 1795 at Mt. Holly, Rutland Co., VT, m 18 Nov. 1818 at Mt. Holly to Isaac Dickerman, d 07 Nov. 1826 in Illinois.

  + 4.   Rhoda[2], b 06 Dec. 1798, m 10 Dec. 1818 Lawson Earl, d 19 Dec. 1882.

2.   Hoxey[2] Barber Jr. (Hoxxey[1]) was born 06 Dec. 1791 at Mt. Holly, VT, etc.

4.   Rhoda[2] Barber (Hoxxey[1]) was born 06 Dec. 1798 at Mt. Holly, Rutland Co., Vermont; m Lawson Earl 10 Dec. 1818 at Mt. Holly, VT, died 19 Dec. 1882 at Mt. Holly, VT.

FIVE

Squeezing Every Bit of Information From Every Record

Most researchers do not fully utilize the records they acquire. Understanding how and why the record was created can help you understand the information provided. We would all like to believe that censuses, vital records, etc. were created just for us to use when tracing our heritage. This could not be further from the truth. Understanding this fact will save you much frustration. The census, for all of the wonderful information it provides, was instituted to count the population for taxes and to reapportion the seats of the U.S. House of Representatives. This explains why only the heads of households were listed by name in the early census schedules (1790-1840) with everyone else tallied. The government was only interested in how many residents, male and female in specified age groups, lived within the given district. Their names were unimportant for the purposes for which the census would be used. By 1820, the government added a column to indicate how many males were between the ages of 16 and 26. This was done to determine how many men of military age resided within a given community or area.

Each new census schedule added columns, subjects, and questions so the government could extract certain statistical data regarding the population. As you look at census records, ask yourself why the census taker (called the enumerator) would ask that particular question. There is always a governmental or tax reason for it. In the 1850 and later census records, the person is asked to supply his place of birth. Since this additional question was added around the time of the heavy Irish and German immigration, the government could now extract statistics on which immigrant groups were concentrated in what areas.

The 1850 and 1860 census years also saw a special census for slaves to determine their distribution throughout the United States. Remember that every census and question had a purpose beyond family history. Knowing this purpose can help you more accurately evaluate the information you obtain.

A special census taken in 1890, along with the regular census, was for veterans and their widows only. The government was able to then determine how many veterans or widows of veterans, from the Civil War and War of 1812, were still living and collecting pensions. This veteran's schedule was another lucky break for the researcher. The regular 1890 census was all but completely destroyed in a fire in January 1921 at the Commerce Building in Washington, DC. Less than 1 percent of the census survived the devastation. The veteran's census survived alphabetically through all of the states, starting with half of Kentucky and continuing to the end of the alphabet. For this reason, this special census has seen more use than other special censuses by the genealogical and historical researcher. All of the census schedules, whether it be the population, slave, veterans, agricultural, or industrial census, should be researched. They all offer different information that can prove useful.

The Census Book: A Genealogist's Guide to Federal Census Facts, Schedules, and Indexes, by William Dollarhide (see the bibliography for additional titles), explains every census, what it contains, where to access it, and what indexes exist, to name just a few subjects. Again, thoroughly learning about the record you will be researching pays off in many ways.

Reminder

TEN QUESTIONS TO "ASK" EVERY DOCUMENT

1. Why was the document created in the first place?

2. Are you looking at the original or a copy?

3. To whom does the document pertain?

4. How close to the original event was the document created?

5. Who are the witnesses, informants, or other persons mentioned in the document?

6. Do you fully understand all of the information and wording in the document?

7. Are any relationships stated or implied?

8. Did the person executing the document sign with a signature or mark?

9. Is the information reliable, usable, or simply clues to further research?

10. What is the full citation for the document?

Reading between the lines is a talent worth perfecting. Ask the document a series of questions. Many types of records provide clues that are often overlooked by the researcher. Don't simply read the words; you must understand their meaning. What was the purpose for the information? What other leads does the information present to you? How else can you use that piece of information? Be creative. There are really no right and wrong answers. You are only limited by your creativity and imagination. Think like a detective and pursue all leads. My job, before I became involved in genealogy, was as a debt collector for a local bank. I apply much of the training I received in that position when researching my family. I am still looking for people—they are just a little less active in evading me!

When the researcher obtains copies of records, either via mail or from photocopies, she must extract every piece of valuable information from the document before moving on to another document. **One way to do this, and I highly recommend it, is to completely transcribe the document, not just abstract it.** This applies to all handwritten documents. Typed documents should be read and dissected as detailed before, but do not really need to be retyped as a transcription. I do retype them into my note field in the genealogy program I use and attach an information card to the upper corner before filing. Abstractions have their place, but not until you transcribe or thoroughly dissect the record first.

Research Tip

Here is an example of an information card:

Document type: _____	Date of document: _____
Full citation:_____	Date viewed:_____
Individual's name:_____	# of pages: _____
State, county, & town named:_____	
Transcription done?_____	Abstract done?_____
Pedigree chart # & person #:_____	

I find that by doing a *complete* transcription of the document and then abstracting the important information, I am less likely to miss an important detail. Human nature allows us to understand the basic document we are reading, whether or not we read every word. Some of those words, when we are forced to decipher them, turn out to be important facts. Terminology has changed over the centuries, and you may not understand what a fairly common term means in an old document. Those of us over thirty or so have heard the expression, "You sound like a broken record." Teenagers today, never mind in the next century, have little or no knowledge of record albums or understanding of that phrase.

Old handwriting styles also pose a whole new set of problems. When you are working in town records, you have the advantage of being able to look at other documents written by the same clerk to compare the style of handwriting. When you cannot make out a letter or word in a document, search other pages to see if you can find words that begin or contain the same letter to see how the clerk formed the letter. This is especially helpful when

Step By Step

TEN STEPS FOR EFFICIENTLY AND COMPLETELY DISSECTING A DOCUMENT

1. Invest in several types of dictionaries.

2. Familiarize yourself with the handwriting styles of the clerk and time period involved.

3. Determine the relationships between the parties involved.

4. Type a preliminary transcription into your word processor, leaving blanks for unknown or unreadable words or phrases.

5. Get copies of several similar documents from the same clerk or locale for comparison.

6. Check for any references to locations, occupations, education, etc.

7. Understand the document and the reason it was created in the first place.

8. Make sure you know if it is an original document or merely a copy of the original.

9. Be observant and careful with all punctuation in the original document.

10. Do a complete and thorough transcription of the document and then an abstract of pertinent information.

using the census. Since certain names are fairly common within a geographical area, and given names are repeated far more often than we would like, you can look for a name containing the letter in question and compare it. Capital letters seem to pose the most problems. T, I, J, and F are commonly mistaken for each other depending on the style of the handwriting. This is especially frustrating when the letter in question is only an initial. You have nothing else to base an educated guess on. If you think the letter might be a T, look for other names, such as Thomas, Theresa, or Thompson, and compare it to the letter in question. In the case of a capital I, look for the names Isaac or Isabel. If it doesn't look like the writer's other Ts, Fs, or Js, and you cannot find a name beginning with I to compare it to, then perhaps it is an I. Whenever you transcribe anything, remember that it is only *your* interpretation of the document. Another transcriber might see something completely different. Ask someone else to take a look at it. Don't ask, "Does this look like an F to you?" but rather "What does this look like?" Many of us will see what we think should be there or what is suggested to us, rather than looking at the record in a totally unbiased manner.

Keep in mind that a *complete* transcription includes *everything* that appears on the document, including all witnesses and whether or not the people signed their names or made their "mark" in place of the signature. Every single word is a piece of information that you may need later. If there are parts that seem to defy transcription, you must indicate this in your typed record. Inserting an ellipsis (. . .) indicates that there are words missing in the transcription. Another way to indicate your inability to read a word or phrase is to include the word "illegible" or a question mark in brackets, for example, [illegible] or [?]. Some transcribers use [*sic*] to indicate a word that has been transcribed exactly as written and is spelled incorrectly. Since a transcription should always contain the exact, even if incorrect, spelling, there should not be too many occasions to use [*sic*] in the transcription. I use it when referring to something besides a misspelling, such as a person's name that might, according to my belief, be incorrectly listed, or in the case of double wording (the land is is [*sic*] located . . .). By keeping the transcription true to the document to the best of your ability, you will be maintaining its integrity as a source of information.

Antiquated words, abbreviations, and terms will cause you many frustrating moments. Understanding these items, as well as the handwriting styles from different eras, geographical areas, and individuals will be helpful in many different ways. **There are several books and pamphlets written on the subject of handwriting.** *Reading Early American Handwriting*, **by Kip Sperry, is an overview of the subject that can be a great help when tackling this problem.** Once you get the hang of American writing, why not move on to European? That opens a whole new can of worms!

Printed Source

An example of an antiquated or specialized term appeared in a will that I was transcribing. The document, which I had hoped would identify the children of the deceased, did not specify the relationships of the people mentioned. The deceased gave several men, bearing the same surname, property. Were they his sons? Were the other surnames mentioned perhaps the husbands of his daughters? There was not enough information to come to that conclusion. Or so I thought. Upon doing a complete transcription of the will, I came across a word that I was unfamiliar with and could not make out (partially due to the handwriting). I left a blank space in my typed transcription and continued with the document. As I continued, I discovered that the word showed up several more times, always when describing a piece of land. It appeared to read "mowly," perhaps a term used to describe the particular piece of land or its purpose. Because the word was written several times, I was able to make out several probable spellings for it. Not being familiar with the word, despite the various spellings I had presumed, I decided to look it up in the dictionary. I was sure that the first letter was an m and the second letter an o or an a. It contained an l or a t depending on which handwritten version I looked at.

Case Study

After looking in several genealogical dictionaries and then a general reference dictionary, I finally found the word. The word was "moiety" and means an equal part or one of two or more equal parts. It is a term that lawyers use even today. With this term now being identified, I realized that the three people mentioned as receiving a "moiety" of the deceased's land were probably his children since they received equal shares. Further research proved this fact and also provided the name of the daughter's husband (one of the three other surnames listed in the document). Since this man also received a moiety of the deceased's land, and women did not often hold land in their own names, her husband was willed her share. This was just one of many cases where a transcription has given me more information than an abstract would have. The word, in the context of the document, did not appear to be as important as the names, but proved to be one of the most important words when taken in the context of the document.

Having a good genealogical, general, or law dictionary, or several of them, on hand while you transcribe documents will be a valuable timesaving tool. Forcing yourself to understand and transcribe every word is a beneficial habit to learn. I have never been disappointed when I expend a small amount of time and effort to understand a word or phrase.

Once you have transcribed the document, preferably on your word processor, you can print it out and staple a copy to the actual document. You will quickly be able to refer to the document without having to deal with the "chicken-scratch" handwriting again. Then, and only then, should you create an abstract of the document. Be sure to transfer the information to the pedigree charts and family group sheets. I have found that I can get several abstracts pertaining to one individual or family onto one sheet of paper. I can then include that page of abstracts in the appropriate binder, along with the family group sheets. There is no need to carry the entire document and transcription with you, since you have gleaned the information from it already. It should be put in your files where you can refer to it in the future. By following this procedure with all of your documents, you will get the most information from them.

There are a variety of documents for the researcher to utilize. Some will provide more information than others. Every document or record should present at least one "clue" to another type of document or record that you need to search. There are certain documents that I use more often than any other because of the clues they present.

Two such documents are newspaper death notices and obituaries. Death notices are usually submitted to the newspaper by the funeral home or undertaker handling the affairs and are pretty basic. The obituary is more like a news item and may be written by a family member or the newspaper staff (based on a form the undertaker fills out and sends to the paper), but usually contains more information. While death notices and obituaries have evolved from nonexistent to rather elaborate biographies over the years, they have always (when available) provided valuable data. Many death notices contain at least the name of the deceased, place of services or burial, and sometimes survivors' names. Obituaries will many times list the deceased's parents, his mother's maiden name, names and residences of living relatives, places of employment, occupations, hobbies or pastimes, military history, or awards won. The list goes on and on. Every piece is valuable to the overall puzzle. Every

Timesaver

DOCUMENTS OR RECORDS THAT ARE THE MOST PRODUCTIVE

1. Newspaper obituaries, death notices, and social columns

2. Census records—state and federal

3. Biographies

4. Wills and probate records

5. Naturalization and passenger list records

6. Local and ethnic newspapers

7. Diaries

8. Vital records—birth, marriage, death

9. Religious records—baptisms, marriage banns, confirmations

10. Land and property documents

person or organization a person came in contact with during his lifetime potentially has records that may be of interest to you. Invest the time to dissect every obituary and death record to see what you can get.

One valuable mention in the obituary or death notice is the name of the undertaker and church where the services were performed. At one time, funerals were held in the deceased's home or the home of a relative. The death notice most likely listed a pastor, clergyman, or church. If only the clergyman's name is mentioned, you can use the city directories, or local newspapers from that time period to determine his church affiliation. This applies to clergymen listed on any certificate, be it a baptism, christening, or marriage. The same city directories can be used to determine what churches and cemeteries existed in the area when your ancestor lived there.

The same technique applies to the undertaker on the record. It has been my experience that funeral homes rarely go out of business, but are absorbed or consolidated with another home in the vicinity. It may take a little leg-work, by writing or calling, to locate the new funeral home, but it will be worth the effort. Again, the local directories and newspapers will point out what other funeral homes were in existence at the time when the other one closed. This, of course, would be more difficult to determine in a metropolitan area like New York City than in a smaller town or city.

As for funeral home records, some undertakers have kept the older records, and others have not. Their records can be informative or brief, but I have always found them to be interesting. I have a record from the undertaker who officiated at my great-grandfather's funeral in 1929. It is rather amusing. The bill reads:

HALL & CROTEAU
Successors to Clinton COLLINS

House Furnishers & Undertakers

WALL PAPER AND SHADES   MARBLE AND GRANITE CEMETERY WORK

Insurance	Victrola Agency
Casket	$150-
Pine Box	12-
Embalming	15-
Hearse to Walpole	30-
Services	10-
Grass & Device	12-
Opening Grave	8-
	$237.00

This bill was included in the Civil War pension file for my great-grand-father and was quite enlightening. I don't know why he needed a pine box and casket, but my grandfather was billed for them. This record is an example of the type of document that did not give me any additional information regarding my ancestor, but was of great interest to me nonetheless.

In many of the old New England towns, there are small family cemeteries dotting the landscape. I have found that the local, currently operating funeral homes have staff who are aware of the burial grounds within the town. They are pleasant to talk to and can answer questions regarding burial customs and rituals.

Another fact that often appears in these notices is the place of internment or burial. That should lead you to the cemetery to see what records they have. Who else is buried in that plot? Who purchased or owns the plot? What plots have others with the same surname? Who is buried on either side of your ancestor? Was or is the cemetery affiliated with any particular church or organization? Many of these questions can be answered by calling or writing to the cemetery office. If you can visit the cemetery when the office is open, be sure to ask the same questions. If the only time you can visit is on the weekend or in the evening, take a look at the stone to see what clues it offers in addition to the previous information. Are there any fraternal (Masonic, Odd Fellows, etc.) symbols adorning the stone? These are all questions that are relevant to your search.

While you are looking at the newspapers for the obituary or death notice, remember to look for a possible article regarding the funeral or death. If the death occurred as a result of an accident, murder, or questionable circumstances, there may be extensive information in the news portion of the newspaper

Research Tip

but no death notice at all. A death that occurred under unusual circumstances might lead you to the coroner's inquest or medical examiner's records. If the death was the result of a crime, the court records should also be searched for details presented during a trial. Many local newspapers listed the names of the people who sent flowers or came from a distance to attend the funeral, and other such newsworthy items. I have even found notes of thanks submitted by surviving family for the flowers and support during their bereavement. As long as you have the roll of film on the reader, or have traveled to the repository that houses them, why not glean every possible detail from them? This is an occasion when "browsing" is a lot of fun. What was happening in the world, state, or town during the time frame that your ancestors were there? What was the prevailing attitude of the population? What is being advertised in the papers? It can all be very interesting and will provide you with other clues and possibilities for further research. If nothing else, you will have a better understanding of your ancestor's lifestyle and era.

Newspapers can also be of interest in times of celebration within the family. If older family members lived to celebrate a one hundredth birthday or fiftieth anniversary, there may be an article in the local paper. Any milestone in your ancestors' lives, such as graduations, ordinations, or promotions might have been newsworthy. Check these milestone dates to see what you find. Unfortunately, some of our ancestors actually show up in police blotters or court postings in the papers. There are times I wish my mother's ancestors weren't just farmers who minded their own business. Some of the criminals got wonderful write-ups in the papers. The saying, "Want to have your family tree researched? Run for office!" is so true. Reporters went all out to get information on the notorious among them and wrote their articles with such flair.

This approach to documents has been referred to as the "Doberman approach." That simply means you latch on to a fact and don't let go until you've gotten everything out of it. Don't let yourself be satisfied with just obtaining the document. That's only the beginning of the search. Utilizing every single scrap of information as a clue to other research will pay big dividends. Once you have the document in your hands, use the other tools (Internet, mail, libraries) to further your research. Be a detective, and don't give up.

\di'fin\ *vb*

Definitions

SIX

Utilizing Research Facilities

THE NATIONAL ARCHIVES

There are several research facilities that all genealogists will use at one time or another. The first such facility is the National Archives and Records Administration (NARA), on the Web at <http://www.nara.gov>. This governmental agency houses copies of all surviving U.S. federal census schedules. In addition to the census, NARA holds the following:

- passenger arrival lists
- naturalization records
- army service records
- naval and marine service records
- volunteers' service records
- military pensions records
- bounty land warrant records
- records of civilians during wartime, American Indians, African Americans, merchant seaman and civilian government employees
- land, claims, and court records
- other miscellaneous records

Is it any wonder that genealogists are never really finished with the National Archives? No matter what stage of the research process you are in, the NARA facilities will have some record of interest to you. I have been researching at NARA for more than ten years and have barely scratched the surface of the wealth of information they hold. Someone once said to a friend of mine, "Why are you going to the Archives again? Weren't you already there?" I don't think there has ever been a facility that I could not use another trip to at one time or another. Every set of parents you discover provides two more problems to solve. It is never ending, but so much fun!

The NARA facility is at Pennsylvania Avenue at Eighth Street NW, Washington, DC 20408; (202) 501-5400. It is the central location for all records held by the governmental agency. Many records that have *not* been microfilmed are held in the Washington, DC facility, including the Civil War pension and service records for Union soldiers, or the regional facility that pertains to the geographical region. Indexes to these pension records are microfilmed and available at some of the regional branches, but the actual pension files are only available in Washington.

There are sixteen NARA Regional Record Services facilities around the country. (See <http://www.nara.gov> for more detailed information, including hours and directions.) They are at the following locations:

National Archives, Southeast Region (Atlanta)
1557 St. Joseph Ave., East Point, GA 30344-2593; (404) 763-7474
Serves Alabama, Florida, Georgia, Kentucky, Mississippi, North Carolina, South Carolina, and Tennessee.

National Archives, Northeast Region (Boston)
Frederick C. Murphy Federal Center
380 Trapelo Rd., Waltham, MA 02452-6399; (781) 647-8104
Serves Connecticut, Maine, Massachusetts, New Hampshire, Rhode Island, and Vermont.

National Archives, Northeast Region (Pittsfield, Massachusetts)
100 Conte Dr., Pittsfield, MA 01201-8230; (413) 445-6885
Microfilm reading room serves primarily the Northeast, but has census, military, and other records of national scope.

National Archives, Great Lakes Region (Chicago)
7358 South Pulaski Rd., Chicago, IL 60629-5898; (773) 581-7816
Serves Illinois, Indiana, Michigan, Minnesota, Ohio, and Wisconsin.

National Archives, Rocky Mountain Region (Denver)
Bldg. 48, Denver Federal Center, West Sixth Ave. and Kipling St., P.O. Box 25307, Denver, CO 80225-0307; (303) 236-0804
Serves Colorado, Montana, North Dakota, South Dakota, Utah, Wyoming, and holds most New Mexico records.

National Archives, Southwestern Region (Fort Worth)
501 West Felix St., Building 1, Forth Worth, TX 76115-3405; (817) 334-5525; P.O. Box 6216, Fort Worth, TX 76115-0216
Serves Arkansas, Louisiana, New Mexico, Oklahoma, and Texas. (Note that most New Mexico records are in the Denver facility.)

National Archives, Central Plains Region (Kansas City)
2312 East Bannister Rd., Kansas City, MO 64131-3011 (816) 926-6920. Serves Iowa, Kansas, Missouri, and Nebraska.

National Archives, Pacific Region (Laguna Niguel, California)
24000 Avila Rd., First Floor, East Entrance, Laguna Niguel, CA 92677-3497; P.O. Box 6719, Laguna Niguel, CA 92607-6719.
Serves Southern California, Arizona, and Clark County, Nevada.

National Archives, Pacific Region (San Francisco)
1000 Commodore Dr., San Bruno, CA 94066-2350; (650) 876-9001. Serves Hawaii, Nevada (except for Clark County),

Northern California, American Samoa, and Trust Territories of the Pacific Islands.

National Archives, Northeast Region (New York City)
201 Varick St., New York City, NY 10014-4811; (212) 337-1300
Serves New Jersey, New York, Puerto Rico, and the Virgin Islands.

National Archives, Mid-Atlantic Region (Center City Philadelphia)
900 Market St., Philadelphia, PA 19107-4292; (215) 597-3000
Serves Delaware, Maryland, Pennsylvania, Virginia and West Virginia.

National Archives, Mid-Atlantic Region (Northeast Philadelphia)
14700 Townsend Rd., Philadelphia, PA 19154-1096; (215) 671-8005. Serves Delaware, Maryland, Pennsylvania, Virginia, and West Virginia.

National Archives, Pacific Alaska Region (Seattle)
6125 Sand Point Way NE, Seattle, WA 98115-7999; (206) 526-6501
Serves Idaho, Oregon, and Washington.

National Archives, Pacific Alaska Region (Anchorage)
654 West Third Ave., Anchorage, AK 99501-2145; (907) 271-2441.
Serves Alaska only.

National Archives, Great Lakes Region (Dayton)
3150 Springboro Rd., Dayton, OH 45439-1883; (937) 225-2852
Serves Indiana, Michigan, and Ohio.

National Archives, Central Plains Region (Lee's Summit, Missouri)
200 Space Center Dr., Lees' Summit, MO 64064-1182; (816) 478-7089. Serves New Jersey, New York, Puerto Rico, and U.S. Virgin Islands.

Each of these regional facilities will have *all* of the U.S. federal census schedules for the entire country, as well as the revolutionary war pension and other microfilmed military records. Each facility holds unique records for the geographical area it serves. These records include naturalization records, federal court records, passenger lists, and other records pertaining to that region.

Each of these regions has a free booklet describing their particular holdings. You can write or E-mail to request one of these informative booklets for the regional office of interest. **You can also visit the NARA Web site at <http://www.nara.gov> and click on "Regional Records Services Facilities" to see what specific records that facility houses.** I am amazed at the number of records housed in our local facility that I have never even touched. Census, naturalization, and passenger lists make up the bulk of the records used for research by genealogists. These records are just the tip of the iceberg. Knowing what records are held in each location may provide new avenues of research that you had not considered. You cannot ask to look at records if you do not know they exist.

Internet Source

Other publications available through the National Archives, for a nominal fee, cover a wide range of topics. The prices and description of each is listed on the NARA Web site. These include:

Military Service Records
American Indian Records
Federal Court Records
Black Studies
Immigrant and Passenger Arrivals
The 1790-1890 Federal Population Censuses
The 1900 Federal Population Census
The 1910 Federal Population Census
The 1920 Federal Population Census

The books listed above are catalogs of information regarding what is contained in specific record types, availability, and microfilm series numbers as well as specific microfilm roll numbers for the films. They explain many of the records and give additional information that is helpful to the researcher. Again, knowing as much as possible about the records you will be using will make your research more efficient.

Two other books available at the NARA facilities, but also available elsewhere are

200 Years of U.S. Census Taking: Population and Housing Questions, 1790-1990
Guide to Genealogical Research in the National Archives

The first is an extensive overview of the entire census history, including what questions were asked, why, and what instructions were given to the census enumerators. Knowing what to expect and having realistic goals will save you much disappointment later.

STATE RESEARCH FACILITIES

State Archives

Another much-used facility will be the state library in any locality of interest to you. Many states also have a state historical society and possibly a state archives. The state archives is the local version of the National Archives. NARA houses documents related to the federal government, while the state archives hold state government and sometimes county government records. This can get confusing at times, since many records are created and stored at all levels of government. Some naturalization and passenger lists, for instance, are state rather than federal records. Before the creation of the Immigration and Naturalization Service, all of these documents and rules pertaining to them were controlled by each individual state. Because of this, documents will vary greatly on what information they provide. After 1906, the federal government provided a standard form for all agencies that were able to naturalize citizens and a more uniform document now exists.

Library/Archive Source

This does not mean that all naturalizations were federal documents after 1906. Quite the opposite is true. The classification of the document (as federal or state) depended on whether it was a federal or state court that actually processed the paperwork. Naturalization records processed in a state or local court would be state documents. These courts may include police courts, superior courts, courts of common plea, circuit courts, supreme judicial courts, and county courts, and can make finding the record difficult at times. Check the town your subject lived in to see if they registered to vote or appeared on a voter list. If they did, then they were likely naturalized citizens, but many fraudulent cases exist. Some of the municipalities still have the voter registration cards that state when and where the person received citizenship. A useful source for determining locations of records is *Guide to Naturalization Records of the United States* by Christine K. Schaefer (Baltimore, Md.: Genealogical Publishing Co., Inc., 1997).

State Libraries

The second group of facilities are the state libraries. State libraries hold a wealth of information from the history of the state, counties, and towns, to indexes of vital records, family genealogies, copies of federal and state census records, and much more. Before you go traveling from one town to another to research, check out the state library and historical society.

Many such facilities have brochures or entire books available that outline their collections. Some have Web sites with online catalogs and finding aids. Most genealogical reference books such as *Redbook*, *The Source*, or *Handybook* contain some information on the state libraries around the country. Make sure you know what they hold before you tackle them. They can be overwhelming at times.

State Vital Records Offices

The third facility that most genealogists will need at one time or another is the state department of health or vital records bureau. Most states currently have statewide registration of all birth, marriage, and death records. On the whole, most did not require statewide registration until 1900 or later. Some states required transcriptions of all records held at the county or local level to be sent to the state office, while others only required it "from this day forward." Bearing in mind that the state copies are secondary sources and not the original record, use the state indexes when you don't know the actual locality of the original. By looking at the state level, you can determine which county or town submitted the record and then look at both the state copy and the original. Remember that the state may have a standard form that the local clerk filled in. This form may or may not include all of the information on the original record. By comparing the state copy to the original, you will be assured that any transcription errors are evident and you have all of the possible information available.

Always check to see if the statewide indexes or records are available at the state library or archive. Many times the earliest of these records are available, but

Timesaver

the more recent ones have restrictions for privacy reasons. There are actually some states that completely prohibit access to the records, while others require that you state your relationship to the individual named in the record and your reason for requesting it. Every state in the union makes its own rules, so learning these rules is important to your success.

One such example is Connecticut. This state requires that you be closely related to the individual in the record to obtain a copy. The state library has indexes to the records through 1850, while microfilming of the records to 1900 is underway, but access to later records is restricted to immediate relatives and members of genealogical societies incorporated in Connecticut (only specific societies are listed). The same rule applies whether you go to the state or town level. The town clerks are instructed to ascertain that you are a member of one of the named societies before allowing you to see the record. Knowing and understanding these regulations, and perhaps joining an approved society before you attempt the research, is crucial. Read anything you can find and make sure the information is current before you take a trip to that state for research. Calling or writing to the state library and asking for specific requirements can help you avoid a lot of frustration. Most, although not all, state libraries have Web sites listing their rules and regulations. Do your homework.

State Historical Society

The fourth facility that most researchers will use is the state or local historical society. These organizations vary greatly from locality to locality. Some are very active, hold large collections of materials, and maintain Web sites, while others are very restricted by time and volunteer effort. I always start with the state historical society since it has a larger collection that covers not only the counties and towns, but an overview of the state as well. Historical societies may or may not collect material regarding genealogy and will concentrate their collections on documents and information of an historical nature. This is not to say that families aren't mentioned in these holdings. Most state and county histories have names of early settlers and members of the community who served the town, churches, and military in the given geographic area. **The novice researcher in favor of the more commonly used vital records often overlooks historical documents.** In most cases, a death record from the early 1800s will not list a place of birth, while a sketch of early settlers in a county or state history commonly names the former state or area of residence. The names of other early settlers, their former residences, and settlement patterns will also provide clues to your ancestor's migratory patterns. Always look at other individuals and groups living in the same area as your ancestor for clues of origin. **Most people did not migrate by themselves, but rather moved in groups or in waves from one location to another.** Early settlers in a new area would often write letters to relatives who stayed behind, extolling the virtues of the new settlement. This would then encourage others to follow at later dates. Utilizing the county and state histories will

Warning

Important

provide you with a more thorough understanding of the time and place in which your ancestors lived.

First you must locate these facilities in your area of interest; determine what they hold either by writing, using the Internet, or calling, and then see if any of these materials are available to you locally or through the Family History Library microfilms. Obtain any pamphlets or publications pertaining to the facility and its holdings to determine if a trip there is worthwhile. If the state historical society has an active Web page, see if the catalog is available; what, if any, records are already posted on the site; and what information about other facilities in the area may be offered.

LOCAL LIBRARIES, SOCIETIES, AND RECORD OFFICES

The fifth, but certainly not the last, facility you will use will be the local library, historical society, or town or county records office. Eventually you will want to get down to the local level and visit the hometowns of your ancestors. This is where you will find truly unique records. Even if you find cemetery transcriptions of the burial grounds and documentation of your ancestor's tombstone, nothing compares with visiting the site personally. Seeing and getting photographs of the homes they lived in, walking the same streets they walked, and getting to feel the area can be very rewarding. Visiting these local facilities and talking with people who are knowledgeable about the local history can provide many new clues and avenues for research.

Case Study

While I was visiting a sleepy little Vermont town one fall, I came across a cemetery on the side of the road near where my ancestor's farm was located. It was lunchtime and the fall color was spectacular, so I decided to take a break and enjoy a stroll through the cemetery. Since I am always prepared, I had in my trunk a bright orange scarf, vest, and hat, a necessity in Vermont during hunting season. After donning my "I'm not a deer" uniform, I enjoyed a quiet lunch and stroll that paid huge dividends. While casually reading the stones, I noticed several surnames that appeared in collateral lines within my family. These surnames seemed somewhat out of place as I had never had any indication that any of them resided in Vermont. I took ample notes from the tombstones, drew a map of the placement of the stones, and took several pictures of the cemetery. Upon my return to the town hall, I inquired about the death records for the individuals in question. To my surprise, they were indeed relatives, although somewhat distant, of my ancestors. Knowing where these "misplaced" families originated made me go back and look at that locale a little closer. I then found additional information on my ancestors, who, to my surprise, had also migrated from the same area, taking my pedigree back several additional generations.

All of the previously mentioned facilities and organizations should be used in any research project you undertake. If your ancestors stayed in one geographical region, unlike others who never seemed to settle down, you will become quite knowledgeable with those facilities and their holdings. I am on a first-name basis with the staff at several state vital records facilities.

When I walk in, the staff says "We've got some new records for you to look at" and then brings me up-to-date on the newest additions. Even if you don't visit the facilities on a regular basis as I do in New England, you can still establish a connection with them through writing or calling.

Another important step is to deposit copies of information with these local facilities, after asking if they accept them, for other researchers to use. Some local organizations maintain a sizeable collection of such papers, which you will not find anywhere else. Some refer to them as family files, or surname files, and they contain amazing information. It may not all be accurate—much of it has no sources cited—but there are many clues to aid in your search. Make sure you label all donations with your name and contact information so other researchers can reach you. I keep a list of the facilities that I have donated materials to in a separate file. If I should move, the telephone company changes my area code, or I change E-mail addresses, I can send a form letter to each organization asking them to update the record. This is just a small step, but very important if you want to correspond with other researchers interested in the same surnames. Many times these files have led to friendships with local researchers that has benefited my research. Having a local contact is a great thing.

Notes

ORGANIZING INFORMATION ON RESEARCH FACILITIES

Once you have determined which facilities you need to visit, prepare a notebook or file on the facility or area. Within this file place any information you come across regarding the facility's hours, holdings, and restrictions; blank forms to be used while there; local maps; and anything pertaining to the area. I also include tourist flyers obtained from the area rest stops. As I have found out, this is valuable when you need to keep your living family occupied while you search for the deceased! These flyers also paid off on one trip when, despite my calling, verifying the hours, closures, and so on, I found the facility closed after driving three-and-a-half hours. I was forced to regroup, visit a few cemeteries, and be a tourist for the day.

The binder I have for each of the New England states includes the following:

- Information on the facility (hours, lunchroom, parking, etc.)
- Flyers of local interest sites
- Maps of the area (many include restaurants and motels)
- Map of the entire state, showing county and town lines
- Photocopies of pages from several reference books pertaining to the facility and the types of record used there
- Blank forms for transcribing records
- Copies of request forms (picked up on a previous visit)
- Page of notes taken on previous trips regarding the pros and cons of the facility
- Empty sheet protectors for inserting any new items I find

TEN QUESTIONS TO ASK A FACILITY BEFORE YOU GO

1. What are the regular research hours?

2. Are there any holidays or scheduled closings that will affect your visit?

3. What restrictions exist that will affect your research?

4. Are records in their original form or in microform?

5. Are the shelves or files open-stack or must materials be paged?

6. Are there restrictions to photocopying?

7. What unique records or manuscripts does the facility house?

8. Is there a particular staff member who is most knowledgeable in your field of interest?

9. Is there public parking, a lunchroom, public transportation?

10. What are the busiest and slowest times at the facility?

This binder or folder still remains fairly compact. For these, I use the report folders that have a place to put three-hole-punched pages. They also usually contain pockets in the front and back covers. By inserting a few empty sheet protectors, you can slide in any additional papers or flyers you find. Remember to keep this folder up-to-date. Facilities will, and do, change their hours of operation depending on the current budget and staff. I always pick up new handouts at every facility to review when I get home. Sometimes the changes on the handouts are minor but will affect your research. Don't just assume that because it looks like the sheet you already have, no changes have been incorporated. Minor changes can make a big difference.

Some facilities require something a little larger than a binder or folder. These facilities, like the National Archives and state libraries, house so many different types of records that a single folder will not accommodate all the information. You can either prepare a tote or briefcase to cover the entire facility, or stick with folders and create subfolders for particular types of records. Do whatever works for you, depending on how you will use it. Make sure to call and verify that the facts you have regarding hours and access have not changed. Always prepare for a trip by establishing your research goals so you will know which records you will use and the folders you need to take. Remember to insert your research plan and a clear list of objectives into the folder before leaving. This is the only piece of paper that should have to be added to the completed folder or binder before hitting the road.

I store these binders on a research shelf in my office. I labeled them for the six New England states and review them on a fairly regular basis. When a new book comes out that covers the research area or facility, I compare the new information to what is contained in the binder and update it where needed. Then I always have the most up-to-date resource for research in that specific area.

PLANNING A TRIP TO A RESEARCH FACILITY

Whenever I delve into a new record type or locality, I begin by compiling and reading as much information as possible regarding the subject. Once I have determined what records the facility holds, as well as what I will need to use, I begin preparing my research goals. I am currently planning my first visit to the New York state library and archives in Albany. First, I visited their Web site and printed out the map, directions to the facility, parking availability, public transportation, places to stay, and general information and publications. Second, I talked with other researchers who have used the facility. Talking to other researchers can be accomplished over the Internet or in person. By subscribing to several mailing lists in the area (New York in general as well as the counties), you will find many researchers who have actually used the facility. Just post a question stating that you will be visiting the state library, historical society, or vital records office, and ask for guidance or tips on the facility. You will be astounded with the replies. One researcher sent me a list of all the New York state census records that are held at Albany, county by county, year by year. You never know until you ask and researchers are a very sharing group of people.

Research Tip

When you have accumulated information on the facility and holdings, decide what records you will need and use once you're there. Try to use as many of the unique records as possible or records that would be costly to obtain or order on microfilm. I am planning to use the New York state census records, since I looked at the years and counties that I would need in the Family History Library film catalog. I would have to order more than thirty rolls of microfilm to get all the towns I need, so I decided it would be more time and cost efficient to go to Albany. I arrived at this conclusion partly because I love to travel, but mostly because of the cost and time involved. Since the census records are only one of the many records that I need, by visiting the state library, I can use several other record types as well, thereby making the trip more than just a luxury. I am combining the trip with a speaking engagement in western Massachusetts. Always think of more than one way to use your time by combining trips.

Another way to save time and money, as well as having a lot more fun, is to travel with other researchers. I have several friends that I travel with whom I met through local genealogical societies. This not only cuts the cost in half, but gives you someone to bounce ideas off of, voice your frustrations, and share your triumphs. You would be surprised how many times they have solved a problem for me just by looking at it from a different perspective. We also discuss our research over breakfast, lunch, and dinner (try doing that with

Money Saver

Idea Generator

For More Info

your spouse), which helps us formulate ideas for further research or a slightly different approach to the problem. Sometimes I find that just hearing myself elaborate on the problem enables me to solve it myself. Having someone just listen to me is a great asset.

When we travel together, we also swap an index card containing the names of our research interests. Since we may be using different types of records within the same facility, knowing the others' surnames gives us two (or more) sets of eyes in every index and record. I have become so familiar with my best friend's family names that I pick them out all the time and make notes for her regarding where I found them, whether we are traveling together or not. We sort of collect each other's ancestors. In all my years of traveling with her, I have never found a connection between our two families, but I am related many times over to her husband. We have traveled locally and as far as Salt Lake City together, and the trips have always been rewarding and profitable. She has visited the massive Family History Library in Salt Lake City many times over the years. I went with her for the first time last year, and it was like having my own personal guide. That's not to say that I didn't feel like a bumbling idiot the first day, but it sure eased my way. All the preparation in the world cannot always smooth the initial encounter in a facility as large as the Family History Library, but I cannot imagine visiting there without a great deal of advance preparation. **The Family History Library and its holdings will be discussed more thoroughly in chapter seven.**

SEVEN

Research Trips: Making Every Minute Count

After you've done as much advance preparation as possible, you are ready to travel to a facility. You should have your binder or folder containing the information regarding the facility and geographic area you will be visiting. You should have prepared a list of objectives and the research you need to accomplish. It is fine to have a large list as long as you understand that you will probably not complete it in one visit. Highlight the "must have" records on your list. These are usually the ones that you cannot get anywhere else. Keep in mind that your first trip to any facility is a reconnaissance mission. You need to actually use the facility before you truly know its advantages and disadvantages.

Make sure you have determined that
- you thoroughly understand the record types you will be using
- the facility actually has the records you need
- the records actually exist for the time period in question
- the records are not available closer to home either on microfilm, online, or by correspondence

Important

When you pack your research tote, remember to include several note-books for taking notes, your research pencil case (see the sidebar on page 92) containing your supplies, your list of research goals, your lunch and snacks if necessary, and your common sense. You would be surprised how many people leave that behind!

When I arrive at the research facility, I open my notebook to the first blank page. I date the page, and document the facility name and location at the top of the page. I know that all notes that follow pertain to that trip's research until I encounter another dated page. This keeps my notes together and organized. This notebook and my research log give me a complete look at the research I did on any given day or location.

I prefer to get photocopies of records rather than take valuable research

Supplies

CONTENTS OF A WELL-STOCKED RESEARCH PENCIL CASE

1. Mechanical pencils, extra leads, and erasers

2. Small stapler with extra staples

3. Colored highlighters, pens, or pencils for marking photocopies

4. Binder clips, paper clips, and rubber bands

5. Small pad of self-sticking notes

6. Coins (35mm film canisters work well for holding these) and good dollar bills for copies, snack machines, and parking meters

7. Hard candy or cough drops

8. Aspirin, headache medicine, and small package of tissues

9. Self-sticking address labels or an address stamp (self-inking)

10. Correction pen or fluid

11. Small plastic magnifying glass

12. Six-inch ruler (for following across lines of print)

13. Blank index cards

Timesaver

Timesaver

time to transcribe or abstract the record while researching at the facility. As a reference librarian, I was amazed at the number of people who use much of their valuable time in a research facility to transcribe information directly into their laptop computer. This saves money on photocopies, but they are shortchanging themselves to save a few cents. I only spend time transcribing a document or entry if photocopies are not allowed or the print isn't as readable as on the microfilm reader. **My time is worth more than the cost of a copy.**

Another advantage to obtaining copies is that I can transcribe them at home or on the commuter train or bus when I am less rushed and can look more closely at the document. How many courthouses or libraries have ideal lighting conditions? If I have trouble reading a portion of the document, I can have another person take a look at it, and they can offer their interpretation of the information. I can also make another photocopy, perhaps on colored paper or enlarged, to maximize the readability. I have found that by highlighting the words in question with a yellow marker and rephotocopying the page, I can make the writing more legible. Try doing that at the courthouse!

By utilizing photocopies, you can do two steps at once. While transcribing the document, log pertinent information on a separate log sheet to compare information (see the example below), and fill in the abstraction form. By logging the information in several different formats, you will find things that might not readily appear when simply transcribing.

NAME	YEAR	CITY	SPOUSE	OCCUP.	WORK ADDRESS/HOME ADDRESS

City Directory Log Sheet

Many times the photocopy of the census page will reveal names that you were not even looking for at the time. I have found information, years after I made the photocopy of the census, when reviewing paperwork. The names meant nothing to me at the time, but now, many research hours later, they do.

Before you can prepare for a research trip, determine what records you need and who holds those records. There is no magical date when all states and territories started to keep detailed birth, marriage, and death records. Every state and territory had their own requirements, starting at different times, for maintaining records. Many states did not begin statewide record keeping until after 1900. That is not to say that records do not exist, only that they are not held at the state level. Some states maintained countywide records rather than in the individual towns. Every state is different, and you must do your homework before you go looking for the actual records.

There are several good books that cover the entire United States in scope and content. Two such books are Ancestry's *Redbook* and *The Source: A Guidebook of American Genealogy*. The *Redbook* lists all the states in alphabetical order, and includes information on the following subjects within the specific state:

- a brief history
- vital records
- federal and state census records
- county and town resources
- local history sources
- land, probate, court, tax, cemetery, church and military records
- map collections
- periodical, newspaper, and manuscript collections
- archives, libraries, and societies within the state
- special focus categories such as immigration, naturalization, African Americans, Native Americans, and other ethnic groups
- dates of county and town formations
- map of the county breakdowns

The Source contains information relating to the different types of records and research subjects that you may encounter. It contains chapters on:

A USEFUL FORM YOU CAN REPRODUCE

For a full-sized blank copy of the City Directory Log Sheet, see page 129. You are free to photocopy this form for personal use.

- The Foundations of Family History Research
- Databases, Indexes, and Other Finding Aids
- Research in Birth, Death, and Cemetery Records
- Research in Marriage and Divorce Records
- Research in Census Records
- Research in Church Records
- Research in Court Records
- Research in Land and Tax Records
- Research in Military Records
- Research in Business, Employment, and Institutional Records
- Research in Directories
- Research in Newspapers
- Ethnic Research, including Immigration, Native American, African American, Hispanic, and Jewish-American Family History
- Tracking Twentieth-Century Ancestors
- Tracking Urban Ancestors
- Tracking Through Heredity and Lineage Organizations
- Appendixes include National Archive Regional Archives System; State Archives; Historical Societies; Family History Library and Its Centers; Genealogical Societies; Where to Write for Vital Records; Selected Acronyms and Abbreviations

Utilizing both of these books will give you a thorough understanding of the records as well as information on where to obtain them. They are valuable tools for the researcher.

Understanding the specific record types, knowing what is and is not contained in them, as well as where to obtain them are some of the best time-savers I know. Reading everything you can find on a particular subject, locality, or research facility will make you more prepared to do the actual research. It won't eliminate every problem, but will certainly give you a more realistic approach to the records.

THE FAMILY HISTORY LIBRARY AND CENTERS

Library/Archive Source

Some great resources for information regarding any state or foreign country are the Church of Jesus Christ of Latter-day Saints (Mormon) Family History Centers, which are located throughout the world. The church has produced research guides to all fifty states and many foreign countries to aid the researcher in determining what records exist for that area. The guides provide not only information pertaining to the specific records, but many include microfilm numbers of films containing the records. These guides are available at any of the 3,200 Family History Centers (FHC) and on a CD-ROM called the SourceGuide (1998), available from the Salt Lake City Distribution Center (1999 West 1700 South, Salt Lake City, UT 84104-4233) and online at <www.Family Search.org>. You can print the research guide or read it directly from the CD. The research guides to foreign countries may include word lists to assist you in translating the records, which will be in the native language.

I have found the guides with word lists to be better than a general translating dictionary. The word lists contain terms that may appear in the foreign records; some are even antiquated terms that will not appear in a current dictionary. Remember that terms found in genealogical records are very different from those you would encounter in the spoken language. They are specialized, so you need a specialized translation.

One example of this was a word I came across in an Italian birth record. The word was "projetta" and the Italian-English dictionary translated it to mean a "projector." The term was actually being used to refer to a foundling child or orphan whose parentage was unknown. Literally, you could take this to mean a child who was thrown, or projected, away. I would have spent a long time trying to figure that one out without the Italian word list available through the Family History Library (FHL).

Once you have determined that the records you need do indeed exist, you must next see if they are available locally or on microfilm through a local FHC. The Family History Centers are scattered all over the United States and the world. The main library is located in Salt Lake City, Utah, and houses millions of rolls of microfilm from all over the United States, Canada, Great Britain, and several other countries. Additionally they have, at another location, thousands of rolls of microfilm of records from other foreign countries. You must request the films stored at the second location in advance of your visit to the Salt Lake City library. All of the films (unless the catalog states otherwise) are available for you to order into any of the FHCs. **To locate a FHC near you, visit the Web site at <www.FamilySearch.org>.**

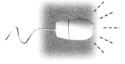

Internet Source

The FHL has been actively microfilming the world's records since 1938 and has made them available to the public at local FHCs. There are currently crews all over the world still microfilming records for inclusion in their enormous collection. If not for the extensive microfilming efforts of the FHL, many of the records we value so highly would be nonexistent or impossible to access. Records are constantly being lost worldwide due to war, earthquakes, other natural disasters, and power struggles. Once these records have been microfilmed, they are available to everyone, even if the originals get destroyed.

Every FHC has the same resources. They all have a complete set of CD-ROMs containing the International Genealogical Index (IGI), Ancestral File (linked pedigrees submitted by researchers over the years), and the FHL Catalog listing all of the books and films held in Salt Lake City. You do not have to be a member of the LDS church to use these services. To be able to research records from all over the world at a local facility is truly incredible. I have never set foot in my grandparents' Italian villages, and yet I have traced both families back to the 1700s using microfilmed records ordered through the FHL.

The IGI contains more than 200 million names extracted from town, county, state, and national records, as well as from records submitted by researchers like yourself. The IGI on CD-ROM is divided into several geographical regions. All of the United States and Canada are included in one set, the British Isles in another, Germany in still another, and other localities have been grouped together in sets. While some will say that the information is questionable, remember that any clue is a valuable clue. Once you have found a record in the IGI, you can determine (perhaps with the assistance of a librarian) what the actual source of the record is. If it is an extraction from a microfilm of town records, that will be indicated. The care used in transcribing these records is excellent. I have never found a mistake in a transcribed record in all the years I have used the IGI.

Important

The Ancestral File, on the other hand, is more prone to errors. Since the LDS church does not have the staff or the time to verify all of the information sent for submission, the resulting records are only as good as the researcher who compiled them. You will have to provide your own sources when you verify the information. This does not mean that you should not consider using the Ancestral File. Just because the state copies of vital records contain errors, do you stop using them? Utilize all of the clues and leads offered to you, no matter where or whom they come from.

The FHL catalog lists the millions of microfilm records that can be ordered through the local FHCs for your personal use. The films are cataloged by locality, so be sure to look up not only the state in question, but the county and town as well. Since records are held by many different governmental and local agencies, you must look under all of the headings, just as you would in a card catalog.

The FHL catalog also lists books that are housed in the Salt Lake City library. Books do not circulate, unless they are microfilmed, so they must be used there. However, just knowing a book exists at all will put you one step ahead. You can get the complete citation from the catalog and then search for the book in a local library or through interlibrary loan. When you find a book in the catalog, read the entry carefully to see if it has been microfilmed. If it has, you can order the book on film through the FHC.

Restrictions apply to some films. The original institution or agency that held the records could put specific restrictions on the microfilms. Occasionally you will come across a film that cannot be circulated to the FHC in your area. This is not dictated by the FHL, but rather by the jurisdiction or owner of the original records.

If the records for the time period and locality that interest you have been filmed, it is best to use the microfilm version, especially if you are unfamiliar with the records themselves. There are several reasons for this. When you order a roll of microfilm from the FHL, it will be sent to your local FHC for your use there. The films must remain in that center since they remain the property of the library. You will have the film for a specified length of time, but you can renew the film if you find that you need more time. You will be able to take your time reviewing the film. Many FHCs are open in the evenings and on Saturdays. This is not true of most town halls or courthouses. **Try to get as much research done as possible from the microfilm and**

Timesaver

save the valuable field research for those records you can obtain nowhere else. As I stated before, using the microfilms for a cursory review of some records can prove to be helpful in narrowing your search on a trip.

Most FHCs worldwide have microfilm printers so that you can make copies of any records you find at minimal cost. The local FHC also has copies of the research guides mentioned before, available for a minimal fee. They may have pedigree and family group sheets and other forms for sale. Each individual FHC will have a unique collection of microfilms on permanent loan to their facility. The size of the facility and the interests of the frequent users of the FHC and/or the volunteer staff members determine the subject matter and extent of these collections.

There is no charge to use the FHC. There is a nominal cost to rent the microfilms and to make photocopies. Since the FHL is a nonprofit entity, everything they offer for sale is at cost.

In March 1999, the FHL launched a Web site that provides access to many of the above resources. Only a small percentage of the IGI is currently online, but more is regularly being added. Being able to use this wonderful database right from home will revolutionize the way genealogists do research. There is still no comparison to using the original records, but narrowing down the search and knowing what is actually available on microfilm is certainly a great start!

When you are ordering microfilms for your research, you must understand how the original records were created. When using the microfilmed town records, in most cases you are looking at the exact papers you would in the town clerk's office or courthouse. Since most town clerks kept specific books for vital records, town affairs, and treasurer's records, they are usually in chronological order within a given volume. Understanding the type of record and *how it was originally recorded* will assist you in determining if the film is of the original or not.

When you are looking at the microfilmed probate records, you will most likely be looking at the copybooks of probates rather than the original packet. There are several reasons for this. When a probate record is originally created, it is filed in what is called a probate docket or packet. These dockets usually contain many small pieces of paper that are accumulated as the process of probate proceeds. Many probates can last for a year or more. I have actually found one that was not completed until fifty-two years after the person died. Every single piece of paper must be reviewed. The smallest detail can be the most important. Look in the margins and on the reverse side of every paper in the probate docket. You may find the one piece of information that will get you through the brick wall! The records contained in the probate packet are usually transcribed into large ledger books by the court clerks. Microfilming these ledger books is much easier than trying to film all of the small pieces of folded paper contained in a packet. Much of the paper is old and brittle and cannot be unfolded and flattened without destroying it. As long as you are aware that you are not looking at the original, it is fine to utilize these films for a cursory review

Case Study

of the records. Once you determine that it is the correct person, you may want to visit the courthouse that holds the originals and look at the entire packet or order photocopies. Be sure to specify that you want copies of both sides of *all* papers included in the packet. There may be enclosures in the probate packet that weren't transcribed into the copybooks at all. Such was the case of one slip of paper contained in Stephen Nichols's probate packet (see case study below).

Case Study: I was researching Stephen Nichols, who died sometime before 1790, which is when his widow remarried. No death or cemetery record was located, so I looked in the probate indexes for Rutland County, Vermont, before 1850. The indexes revealed two probate records for Stephen Nichols—one in 1788 and the other in 1840. Naturally, at first I disregarded the one that was dated 1840, since I knew the widow had remarried in 1790.

The will, which was included in the 1788 record, indicated that Stephen Nichols died between 5 September 1787 and 18 March 1788. I was able to narrow the date of death because the will, written and signed by Stephen Nichols, was dated 5 September 1787 and the widow presented the will for probate on the latter date. This is as close as I have been able to get to an actual death date thus far. The will did not reveal as much as I had hoped. Mr. Nichols stated that, "I will and ordain the same [meaning his estate] be equally shared among my children, which I do give to them their heirs and assigns forever." He did not name or even provide the number or sex of his children.

Since I had no information on how old Stephen was, I couldn't determine how old the children might be. I could estimate his wife's age from subsequent census records and her death record, but were these children his or theirs? The will did not indicate this; he merely stated "my children" rather than "our children." This is a good example of why it is important to read and understand every word. How a person expresses a thought may indicate a clue that you should follow up on. They may very well have been Stephen and Nancy's children, or just his from a previous marriage.

I continued, a bit disheartened, to read the remainder of the probate packet. Included was a small slip of paper dated 24 April 1788, which stated the following:

"April 24, 1788 gave directions to John Stafford & Rowland Stafford to Notify the Creditor to Stephen Nichols Estate to exhibit their claims by the 18th March 1789 to post up an advertisement in Danby and Stephentown State of New York and in the Bennington Papers 3 weeks." Signed E. Clark Judge Probate

This one slip of paper opened up a whole new avenue for research. This family, to the best of my knowledge, had never left New England and the widow remarried in the same town where Stephen and his wife owned land. Not only had I never heard of Stephentown, New York, I had no idea why the court would require posting the notice there. Subsequent research revealed that Stephen Nichols, along with his wife, Nancy Stafford, and her family, had all migrated through Stephentown at some point. I have not found evidence of either family in the Bennington area as yet. When I researched in Stephentown, I also found several other northern Vermont ancestors that had migrated through Stephentown.

Because I am a thorough researcher, I decided to look at the 1840 probate for a Stephen Nichols as well. Perhaps this Stephen would turn out to be a son of the previous one. To my surprise, it was a continuation of the probate record of 1788. This time, the papers named all five of his daughters, who they married, where they lived, and, in two cases, their children as well. The second probate was because one of the daughters, Barbary Nichols, had never married and lived her life with her mother and stepfather, thereby never exercising her right to her fair share of her father's estate. Barbary's mother died in 1840, and Barbary petitioned the court for her share. Since her mother, after she remarried, had given birth to several other children, Barbary must have wanted to be sure they did not share in the original estate division. All of the information contained in this subsequent probate proved that my Druzilla Nichols who married John Carpenter was indeed the daughter of Stephen and Nancy. Due to the 1840 records, I was able to identify all five daughters and determine that there were no surviving sons.

In the case of the Italian civil records, the FHL microfilm was of the original book where the clerk recorded the document. When I sent for a copy of one of the documents, I received the standard filled-in form from the Stato Civile, or town hall. The form contained much less information that I got from the microfilm. Knowing this situation existed allowed me to make the decision to spend the money to order the many (forty-three to be exact) microfilm rolls available through the FHL rather than write for documents from Italy. I spent far less money, although I did work harder, researching the originals on film than if I had ordered them by mail. I also acquired many more records than I would have by writing. I was able to do all of the collateral lines at the same time.

The same holds true for land records. The *original* land deed is given to the person purchasing the land. It is up to that individual to take the document to the appropriate office and have it placed "on the record." In the case of land records, you have no access to the original unless you find them in family papers, so only the copybooks are available. Knowing this can save you a trip to the town or county office to look at the books if they are available on film. Utilizing your on-site research time in an efficient manner is the goal. Use that time to look at unique or unfilmed records, or to compare the original records to the copybooks.

Another way to save considerable time when researching away from home is to see if there are any published or microfilmed indexes to the records. Many probate and land records, especially the earlier ones, have been indexed. I always order a microfilm or check the published indexes first to determine if there is a record for the subject of my research. You can then make a list of all the records, including the volume and page number that you wish to review. This will save you time at a distant facility and make the research process

Timesaver

Timesaver

TEN WAYS TO CUT YOUR LIBRARY STAY IN HALF

1. Research the facility before you plan your visit.

2. Obtain any publications or reference material regarding the facility.

3. Familiarize yourself with the record types you will be using.

4. Be prepared with blank forms, completed indexing, etc.

5. Gather all of the needed supplies for your research trip: notebooks, pencils, stapler, paper clips, and so on.

6. Make verbal contact with the presiding official or staff at the facility.

7. Put all of your materials into a traveling binder and *label everything*.

8. Dress in layers, with pockets.

9. Photocopy all records and information whenever possible to save time on transcription and abstracts.

10. Be pleasant, courteous, and patient with the staff.

---

more organized and efficient. Remember to pay attention to records that, on the surface, might seem too late for your subject. Keep the Stephen Nichols case in mind and look at all of them!

Once you have found the person's record in the index, you can determine if there is enough material to warrant a trip, if you should order the microfilm, or if you want to request the record from the holding facility. Pay special attention to other individuals in the same geographic area and time frame with the same surnames. These might well be siblings, parents, or other relatives of your research subject and can provide additional information on your ancestor. Many times the index has revealed that there is no record in the person's name and a trip would have been wasted. Other times there will be so much that a trip would be less expensive than ordering copies of many records. At this point, if there seems to be an abundance of records that you will need to look at, perhaps due to a common surname in the area, you may decide to order a microfilm from the FHL to do a cursory review. This way you can eliminate the records that are of no interest to you and then concentrate a research trip on the originals of those records.

Sometimes there are other records in the facility, or nearby facilities, that have not been microfilmed. If that is the case, you can determine your personal goals and make a decision about taking a trip or not. By weeding out the nonrelevant records through the use of indexes and microfilms, you will have more time on-site to look at those unique items. Trips can be very rewarding when you take the time to prepare for them. There are several things that should always be done before you travel.

Reminder

First, obtain specific information regarding the facility you will be visiting. The following questions should be answered to your satisfaction:

1. What are their holdings? Determine that they actually have the records for the time frame you are interested in and that they are available for use.

2. Do they have a manuscript collection? Find out what types of special collections they hold that may be of interest to your research goals.

3. What are their rules for access to the records? Some facilities will limit the materials that you can take into the research room with you. Knowing this ahead of time will save you much frustration.

4. Will they make photocopies or will you be required to transcribe the records yourself? Some records are in fragile condition. Knowing ahead of time that photocopies are not allowed will enable you to be prepared to spend more time there than if copies are allowed.

5. What are the hours for *researchers*? Some facilities have business hours and *different* research hours. Make sure you specify that you want the hours that cover research. Are there any local holidays or scheduled closings during your visit?

6. Are there any lunch facilities, or should you bring your own lunch and beverage? Is there a lunchroom available? Is the facility air-conditioned? Are portable computers allowed? If so, are there any restrictions to their use? Are there electrical outlets to plug them into?

7. Is there public transportation to and from the facility? What parking is available?

Second, once you have determined that you will be visiting the facility, you must do some additional preparation. Just as you make airline or motel reservations in advance, determine what you will be researching before you get there!

Tip

1. Review the types of records you will be using. This is a good time to reread the chapter on land or probate records from one of the many books covering the subject to refresh your memory. Many beginner books have chapters on the different types of records. There are also books specific to certain record types such as land, naturalization, and probate. Make sure you know as much as possible about your prospective research.

2. Prepare a sheet of research goals for your visit. List the specific records you will need to look at, listing them by order in year, volume, and page. I make a checklist of all of the records that I intend to use. As I look at the specific record, I mark any notations on this checklist. I will record "five pages photocopied," "abstracted document," or otherwise indicate what I did pertaining to that record. By recording these notes on the research goals sheet, I know exactly what I have and have not completed. I also know how many pages of copies I should have. This list is helpful in keeping you focused on the important records in that facility. It is easy to become overwhelmed in a large, busy facility. Staying focused is crucial. If you should run out of time before you

run out of records to look at (this always seems to happen to me), you will have a completely annotated list to pick up on the next day or visit.

3. Make sure to take along all of the information you need for the trip. This includes everything you accumulated by mail or phone about the facility, including the name of the person you spoke with. Leave your files out on your desk so your spouse can easily find them when you call home and ask them to check for something you forgot!

4. When packing your research materials, be selective and take only what you need. This is one mistake that many researchers make. They take along everything they have. There is only limited room in most research facilities. I have actually seen researchers come into the library or records office with a suitcase on wheels for a few hours of research. Be focused and carry the minimum amount of materials with you. If you want to bring along how-to information about the type of records you will be using, photocopy sections out of the book and add it to the research notebook rather than taking along the whole book. If you are driving, you can be a little more flexible. Leave material you might need in the car (as long as you park fairly close), and you can always retrieve it should the need arise. After several such trips, I realized that I never needed the things in the car, so I started leaving them at home.

5. If your research trip will be part of a family vacation, make sure to pack all of your research materials in a separate tote bag or briefcase. My husband once dropped me off at a facility and as he drove away, I realized I didn't have one of my notebooks that I had packed in my suitcase. I now have a travel tote bag for such trips and everything is packed in it. A friend of mine picked up several nylon zippered bags at a discount store and prepared one for each of the facilities she uses on a regular basis. She has all her supplies for that facility (blank forms, research identification cards, copy cards, maps, etc.) permanently packed. All she has to do is throw in her pencil case, the list of records she wants to research, her lunch, and she's on the road. Either of us can be ready on a moment's notice to go almost anywhere!

ONCE YOU HAVE ARRIVED

Important

1. Stake a claim. Place your notebook or other research items at a seat on one of the designated research tables. **Never leave your pocketbook or laptop computer unattended (or use a locking devise).** If you cannot lock these items up in a locker, keep them with you. I never take a purse to a facility. My wallet is in my briefcase; cash, coin, and credit cards are in my pants pockets or waist pack. You want to focus on the research, not protecting your valuables.

2. Get the lay of the land. Take a brief stroll around the room to see how it is set up. Where is the information desk, copier, rest room, water

fountain? If it is your first time at the facility and they offer a short guided tour, take it. Many questions are answered when taking these tours. I have learned things about the repository that I did not know, leading to more research avenues.

3. Get down to business. Find out where you make requests for materials and obtain any forms that must be used to accomplish this. Are there specific times of day that requests may be made? When is the "last call"? Get out your list of research goals and your research log sheets. If necessary, look up, either in the index or catalog, the records or items you are interested in. Log them on your research log sheet and make your first request. Some facilities limit the number of requests that can be made at one time, so adjust your requests accordingly. Try to make your first requests as soon as possible upon arrival. This serves two purposes. First, make note of the time the request is made, then keep track of how long the retrieval takes. Second, during the wait, you can look up additional items of interest, even if you did your indexing before you came. There may be additional items of interest that you had not considered. When the clerk or librarian returns with the documents you requested, note the time on your research log sheet. Try to do this several times during the first hour or so of your visit. This will give you a feel for how many documents can be retrieved in a given time period. Until you have actually used a facility, you won't know how much time is required to retrieve the records, have copies made, and so on.

4. **Assess your progress about halfway through your allotted research time and prioritize the remaining records to get the most important ones first.** This is an important step to avoid spending too much time on records of lesser importance. I sometimes use colored highlighters to mark the "must have" records on my list. If I have not gotten to them by the halfway mark, I make sure that they move to the top of the list for the next hour. You may need to reassess your goals at this point. Look at what you have already accomplished and how much you still have left. You may have accomplished more than you anticipated, although it usually goes the other way. I almost always find I had more records to look at than time to do it. That's OK on the first few trips. You will get the hang of it and be better able to judge how much you can accomplish after you have visited several different facilities.

Tip

5. Make notes to yourself regarding the facility once you're there. Was it crowded? Was it too warm or cold? How many records were you able to look at in an hour? Were the clerks receptive to your requests? What special rules or obstructions to research did you encounter? This can be done on an index card or sheet of paper in your binder/folder for that facility, and then kept in a file at home. I find it very helpful to review the card from my previous visit before I revisit a repository. This is especially important if you found that it took much longer than anticipated to get the records or have the copies processed. You will

be more prepared the next time you visit the facility. Perhaps, in some cases, it could mean that you prefer to order records by mail rather than spend time there. There are several places like that on my "Did it once, don't want to do it again" list.

6. Keep track of the time. Make sure you are aware of the time, especially when it is one hour from closing time. This is when you look at your list of research goals one last time and request the most important records you need before time runs out. Some facilities will give you a fifteen- or thirty-minute warning, others will not. If you have any "dead" time while waiting for records or copies, review your research log and keep it up-to-date during the day. Also reread your research goals and make sure they have not changed. You may have found information in a record that leads you to another record that is not on your list, but may be important. Always remember to stay focused, but be flexible as well.

THINGS TO REMEMBER WHILE ACCUMULATING INFORMATION

Step By Step

While you are at the research facility, there are certain things you should do that will keep you organized and make it easier to review your materials when you return home.

1. Be diligent about the research log sheet. I cannot stress this enough. You must be able to see a summary of everything you looked at during the day so you will not have to look at it again.

2. When making photocopies from a book, make sure to copy the title page of the book first! The title page contains information including the title, author, place and date of publication, and publisher that will be important to include when fully citing your source. Then copy the pages you need. I prefer to write the needed pages on a piece of paper, rather than sticking little bookmarks into the book. This provides you with a written list of the needed pages and makes it easier to determine if you got the correct ones. Small pieces of paper used to mark the pages can fall out while you are making copies, and it is very easy to miss important pages because they are not marked.

3. Once you have photocopied everything from the book, take the copies and the book back to the table. If the library call number is not printed on the cover page, write it on your photocopy. I also write the name of the facility on the cover page so I will remember where I used the book. Review the page numbers you wanted to copy, making sure that you got all of them. I also highlight the item of interest on the copies, which is another way to doublecheck that I copied the correct pages. Staple the pages together with the cover page on top, note the number of copies on your research log, and put them away.

4. Do not spend time transferring data from the copies into your files or on your charts while at the facility. Use as many books or records as

THINGS TO REMEMBER WHEN PHOTOCOPYING

1. Copy the title page of the book.

2. Record the call number of the book and the facility where it was found.

3. Highlight the pertinent information on the copied pages.

4. Check to be sure that the information doesn't continue to the next page.

5. Staple all of the copies together.

6. Copy any pages that contain explanations of abbreviations contained in the book.

7. Check your research log to make sure you have recorded the search results.

you can while there and save the transcription for later. If you are on a multiday trip, you can review these copies later in your hotel room. If necessary, you can readjust your goals for the next day.

5. If you take a laptop computer with you, avoid the temptation to enter all of the information you find in books or records while at the research facility. I see many people do this, and they spend hours transcribing records that could have been photocopied in less than five seconds for a few cents. Copies are cheap insurance that you get all of the information you need exactly as it was presented. Whenever you transcribe something, whether by hand or typing, it is prone to error. Later when you look at the entry and find an error, you won't know if the error was in the original document or in your transcription. Copies eliminate this. You have an exact duplicate of the information. Don't waste valuable research time doing something that can be done later just to save a few dollars. Remember, your time is money!

6. Pick up any flyers or information sheets that are available about the institution or other local facilities. You can find wonderful local organizations by looking at the "freebie" table in most libraries or governmental offices. Ask the staff if there are any publications for sale that concern your research interests. Many societies publish pamphlets and books on local research topics.

Research trips are always valuable experiences and can provide additional sources for further investigation. Knowing what the facility holds, understanding the record types, and thoroughly preparing your objectives before you go will result in a more enjoyable and successful trip. Following the simple steps outlined in this chapter, until they become second nature, will improve your research skills and results.

Many of these tips are the result of learning experiences from actual research trips, either by myself or other researchers. The basic premise of "always be prepared" can and will be successfully applied to many other aspects of your life. Organization has become more important to me as I have gotten older (my memory isn't what it used to be), and my research time has become more finite. Investing time in advance of a research trip, either by writing, using the Internet, or calling the facility, makes the trip more profitable. Make every precious minute *in* a research facility count, utilize your time wisely, and you will reap the benefits in many ways.

EIGHT

Tapping Into the Knowledge of Others

Timesaver

We are living in a time when there are endless opportunities to attend conferences, seminars, lectures, or workshops. There are many fellow genealogists to learn from as well. Every researcher has encountered unique problems, and possibly found unique solutions to common problems, and they can share that knowledge with others. **Networking with other genealogists, which has become easy with the use of the Internet, is one of the best timesaving tools you have available.** Learning from other's mistakes and successes can be rewarding.

If you are a member of a local genealogical group, you should be able to network with other researchers in your area. If you use the local libraries, you will most likely run into the same people many times. Make friends with some of these people, and everyone will benefit. People, no matter what level of research they are at, have some information worth sharing. As I said before, just verbalizing the problem sometimes results in a solution. I have learned many tips from beginners as well as experts, so don't count anyone out.

Local historical and genealogical societies hold workshops, meetings that feature a speaker or instructor, and programs that may be of interest to you. Watch the newspapers for any lectures that might interest you. Some organizations post these events at the library, especially if they have a special historical or genealogical room for research. Ask the librarians if they know of any groups that may meet in the library or the immediate area. You will be amazed at all that's happenings in your own area!

Tip

One way to keep up-to-date on the genealogical offerings is to become a member of a local, county, state, or national society. In New England, we are fortunate to have the New England Historic Genealogical Society (NEHGS), which is located in Boston. This is the oldest genealogical society in the country and has been in continuous operation for more than 150 years. They publish

Sources

GROUPS OR SOCIETIES THAT MAY ALREADY HAVE THE INFORMATION YOU NEED

1. National Archives and Records Administration

2. Family History Library in Salt Lake City and your local Family History Center

3. Vital records offices—state, county, or town

4. State archives

5. DAR—Daughters of the American Revolution organization

6. Historical societies—state, county, and local

7. Genealogical societies—state, county, and local

8. Surname societies and family associations

9. Libraries—public, state, college, and academic

10. Town halls

11. County courts—probate, land, and vital records

12. Fraternal organizations

13. Ethnic organizations

14. Churches

15. Cemeteries and undertakers

16. Internet

17. Employers

18. Occupational organizations

19. Book publishers—historical and genealogical

20. Military facilities

---

a bimonthly magazine called *New England Ancestors* and the much-acclaimed publication called *The New England Historical Genealogical Register*, more commonly referred to as the *Register*. This society has been in the forefront of the genealogical community for many years.

The collection housed in the library at 101 Newbury Street in Boston is outstanding. Contrary to popular belief, the holdings do not focus just on New England. They hold one of the largest collections for the Canadian Maritimes and the eastern provinces of Canada, including all of the Canadian national census records. They also have a large collection pertaining to the British Isles and all of the United States. They have a manuscript collection that is noted worldwide as being very extensive.

NEHGS's microfilm collection contains most of the vital, town, and land records for all of the New England states. The collection has been expanded almost 100 percent over the last couple of years. Every time you visit, there are new records to research. The two best reasons for becoming a member, in addition to the wonderful research facility, are the knowledgeable staff and the information about programs that are held around the country. The staff members are among the top in the field of genealogical research. Many of them have lectured worldwide on an almost endless list of topics.

The society sponsors many conferences, lectures, and research programs throughout the year all over the United States, Canada, and the British Isles. They have tours to Salt Lake City that include research time as well as instructional lectures and assistance by accompanying staff members. As a member, you will be kept up-to-date, through the magazine or separate mailings, on the activities being held. You will also find mention of other organizations that may be helpful to your research. There are many local and national organizations that cohost some of the NEHGS conferences. It is a great way to keep abreast of the happenings in the genealogical community as a whole.

As mentioned in the chapter on the Internet, you will want to get on several mailing lists in the geographical area of interest. The knowledge that the local societies and researchers will provide you with is almost endless. I have joined several genealogical and historical societies in the counties where I am doing research. These groups have members all over the world along with many local members. The local members have the knowledge of what records are available, where they are located, how you can access them, and may even be able to provide you with information regarding relatives or descendants still living in the area. **(For more information, see chapter four.)**

See Also

One group that I belong to allows you to post your surnames of interest on the list. After doing this, I received an E-mail from a granddaughter of one of my "difficult" individuals. She had information that preceded the vital records of the area, including marriage, death, and burial information that I had never found. We now correspond on a regular basis, providing each other with information the other does not have. She was thrilled to find out that another cousin was researching William B. Miller! Another list member actually had the family Bible for a family I was researching. All of this is out there. Use it!

Using the knowledge of others is one of the best ways to expand your research circle. It is available to you right from home at whatever hour of the day you might have free. Networking has become very easy with the explosion of the Internet. If you take a few minutes to list the different "groups" your ancestors fit into, you will be amazed at the new research possibilities that will arise. **Classifying your ancestors by ethnic group, fraternal or religious affiliation, residence locale (local, county, and state), gender, occupation, military service, time frame or era, social class, and any other classification you can think of will give you ideas of additional records to look for.** I always keep a

Idea Generator

notebook beside my bed to make notes regarding ideas that pop into my mind either in a dream or when I am reading before turning out the light. Since I love historical fiction and genealogical publications, I often come up with ideas when reading and need to write them down when they occur. I am continually amazed at how many times I have solved a research problem in a dream, only to find another avenue of research that I had not considered. OK. So I am addicted to genealogy—there are worse things than dreaming about your ancestors.

If you have research that concerns a specific ethnic group or geographical location, seek an organization that specializes in the subject matter. I belong to the Italian Genealogical Society of America, the Genealogical Society of Vermont, the French Canadian Society, and the Vermont Old Cemetery Association, to name just a few. The members of these organizations concentrate their efforts searching out records that pertain to their group, and they know an amazing amount of information. Many have meetings, conferences, publications, and researchers to assist you. They know what the most recent publications are, what the idiosyncrasies of the records are, and possibly have native speaking members who can provide translations.

Many small, local genealogical and historical societies have regular publications, either in the form of a newsletter or as a continuing series or journal. By subscribing to these publications, all of the new information being released, new publications being sold, and reviews of books and products will come directly to you via the mailbox. Many groups also allow for the posting of queries in their regular publications, while others publish a yearly "members research interest" list. Get involved locally with your historical or genealogical society to meet others with similar interests. Many of these groups organize research trips for their members. Monthly meetings provide a wealth of information, lectures, and networking that you should use to your advantage.

Tip

Another way to learn is by volunteering at a facility that houses records, such as the library or archives facility. You need not be an expert to offer your services. All such facilities offer new volunteers some degree of orientation. Everyone is new at some point, and there is nothing better than jumping in and learning as you go. Using the records or facilities yourself is the best learning tool you have. As you become accustomed to the facility and the specific records they hold, you will be able to assist others. Something as simple as helping another researcher load a roll of microfilm on an unfamiliar reader or printer can make all the difference. I volunteered for four hours each week at a local FHC while working a sixty-hour per week job, maintaining a household, and raising two children. If you volunteer at what you love to do, you will find the time, enjoy yourself, and learn a great deal. Consider it time you take for yourself, doing what you like and learning at the same time.

Organizations that pertain to specific ethnic or religious groups will provide you with information regarding your research interest. The officers and members of these specialized groups are more likely to know the ins and outs of the records that pertain to their ethnic or religious group. They have used the records extensively, many can translate documents for you, and just having another researcher who has used the records can make your search more fruitful.

Local, county, and state historical societies should not be overlooked. Seasoned genealogists know that the social history and ethnic groups of the region are vital to research success. Knowing the history of an area, what groups settled there, what industry existed, and what social groups made up the population can provide many clues for further information. It can also provide you with interesting facts regarding your ancestors and their surroundings. These historical societies have members who have lived in the community for many years and hold a wealth of information that can help you. They may provide you with local folk tales, locations of old farm houses and cemeteries, as well as stories about your ancestors that they heard as children. Local societies may have conducted oral history interviews during the town or county bicentennial celebration or other local celebrations that will shed additional light on the social history of the area. They may have pictures of schools, graduating classes, buildings, and businesses to share with you. The possibilities are almost endless.

Idea Generator

Another resource that is often overlooked by the researcher is the local Council on Aging or senior citizens group. Like the historical society, there are many members within these groups who have extensive knowledge of the town and its early residents. This is especially useful when researching ancestors who lived in the twentieth century. Many of these people may have gone to school with your parents or grandparents, lived in the same neighborhood, or even worked for your ancestors. Many schools are now conducting oral histories of senior citizens within the community. This helps both the younger and older generations understand the changes they have seen in their lifetimes. Better communication develops from these projects. One high school has "Senior Teas" on a fairly regular basis, bringing senior citizens and teenagers together in a social setting. Other communities have students adopt a senior citizen as a "grandfriend" and have regular get-togethers to keep up with each other's lives. These are just some of the ways to tap into the knowledge of the senior members of the community and learn the many wonderful stories that make family history research so rewarding. If you work in the field of education, you could suggest incorporating a similar project into the current curriculum. If you are involved in the parent-teacher organization, as I was when my girls were in school, encourage this type of project within the group. I was pleased at how receptive the parents and teachers were to such ideas. Even though I do not live in a community where my ancestors lived, I have been able to learn from other seniors who lived through the depression, world wars, social and economic pressures. I've also learned about the everyday life that my ancestors experienced.

Spend a few minutes reflecting on the time frame of your ancestors. What was going on in the world or state during their lifetime? Then consider the ways you might learn more about these events through the local and national societies or groups that already exist. Tap into that knowledge and use it to your advantage.

NINE

Research Etiquette: Getting the Most From Research Facilities and Records Offices

Important

Research etiquette is crucial to a researcher's success or failure. How you approach and treat a public official, librarian, archivist, or volunteer makes the difference between a profitable research trip and a frustrating waste of time. Remember the phrase our mothers preached to us, "You only have one chance to make a first impression." This applies to our everyday life, but more importantly to our research. A friend of mine once said, "I'd hate to be the next researcher who asks for assistance after my mother leaves." Apparently her mother was very demanding of the officials who maintained the records she wanted to see. They were not pleased to see her coming.

There are several things you can do, and should keep in mind, when you are researching at a public records office. This includes town and county clerks, courthouses, and cemetery offices. The employees are not there just to serve you. They are there to provide a service to the current residents of their jurisdiction. Town clerks must handle voter registration, animal and hunting licenses, recording of current vital records, local government business, and the other details that keep the local government working from day to day. The same applies to the local and county court clerks and cemetery caretakers. They are busy handling the daily tasks of running their departments.

Understanding that your search for your ancestors will not be as pressing for the local official as it is for you will help you see things from their perspective. One way to make the visit more profitable and pleasant is to call the facility ahead of time. The same rules apply when visiting a town or county office as when you are visiting a research facility specializing in genealogy. Ask the person in charge when the best time is to come. All offices have days that are busier than others. Is there any special time for you to do specific research? Should you make an appointment to use the records? Many times you will discover, when making this initial contact, that the office doesn't even have the records you want. Perhaps they've been transferred to another facility or are restricted and cannot be used. The employees may be able to tell you if the library or historical society has copies of the records you are interested in.

Don't enter a record office less than one hour before closing and expect to be greeted warmly. If you have no other time to go, you might call ahead and explain what records you are interested in, and see if they can be retrieved in advance of your arrival, thereby saving time when you get there. Make sure you are packed up and out of the facility at least five to ten minutes before closing time. Being considerate of the employees will pay off in most instances.

Important

RESEARCHERS' RULES OF ETIQUETTE

1. Remember that your research is not the clerk's priority.

2. Don't enter an office or library within one hour of closing time.

3. Be patient with the staff, and wait your turn.

4. Dress in a businesslike fashion—neat, clean, and professional.

5. Show respect for the records and the staff that maintains them.

6. Leave all books or records in the same, or better, condition than you found them.

7. Be careful in your handling of all documents.

8. If there is no charge for the assistance given you (at churches, historical societies, and cemetery offices), make a small monetary contribution.

9. If you use a facility on a regular basis, consider volunteering or just assisting others while you are there.

10. Learn about the records you intend to use *before* you go.

11. Present a positive attitude and say "please" and "thank you."

12. Always express your appreciation to the staff before leaving the facility.

Reminder

Patience is another skill worth learning and practicing. I have found that many people actually slow down when you try to rush them. Not everyone can be efficient and helpful under pressure. Perhaps my friends' mother has been there right before you arrived. Be courteous, friendly, and patient. Do not relate your entire family history to the clerk—most are not interested.

Be businesslike and professional in your appearance and behavior. I have found that I get a much better reception, as well as a more friendly and efficient clerk, when I am dressed in a professional manner. I don't mean you must

Tip

dress in a suit or dress and heels, but don't just throw on your old grubby jeans, sweatshirt, and sneakers either. You will be amazed at the difference your appearance will make. Think about the kind of first impression you want to make.

I have done several experiments regarding the effect that appearance has on research success. I have gone to the same record office on several different occasions, dressed differently each time. I have always found that if I wear a blazer or jacket, with a neat shirt, and a little jewelry or scarf, I receive a better reception than when I enter in pants and a shirt alone. Many times I have worn the jacket over a pair of nice jeans, and it still works. Being conscious of your appearance can make a big difference. I also carry a briefcase rather than a tote bag on a research trip. This presents a more professional appearance. Being well-groomed makes a great first impression!

The next tip is applicable in some facilities and is not really necessary in others. In New England, we have many research facilities that are scholarly in nature. They are used to dealing with professors, graduate students, and historians rather than genealogists as part of their daily routine. One such facility has a wonderful collection of county and family histories, collections dealing with the maritime trade, and other important historical collections. **The first time I used this facility as a genealogical researcher, I was quite dismayed at the attitude of some of the employees.** After initially asking me the purpose of my visit, they ignored me. They wouldn't make photocopies for me or even retrieve items that I had requested. I was required to pay to have the copies mailed to me, as they "couldn't possibly do them now." It seemed as if they really didn't want me there.

Case Study

After I left, making a note in my book regarding the "adventure," I went home to see if I could figure out what the problem was. After much thought, I decided to return to the library the next week to try out my appearance theory. I dressed in slacks, a dress shirt, blazer with scarf, and carried my research in a briefcase. When I entered the library, I was greeted with a smile and again the inquiry as to the purpose of my visit. Rather than saying "genealogical research," I said, "I am researching early Essex County agricultural families." I was escorted to a table, showed how to fill in a request form for materials, and copies were produced immediately upon my request. I felt like a visiting scholar, and the staff was anxious to assist me. Simply trying a different approach can make the difference. Presenting yourself in a professional and serious manner will generally affect the treatment and service you receive. Try it and see. You have nothing to lose and everything to gain.

Showing respect for the records, as well as the staff, will also make a good impression. Treat all of the records gently, keeping in mind the age and condition of the books or papers. Never use ink pens near original records. I have seen researchers use the tip of a pen or the eraser on a pencil to turn the pages in an old record book. Handle the books and pages gently. Many clerks will watch how you handle the records initially and then decide whether you can be trusted with them on your own. Showing that you have respect for the documents and know the proper way to handle them will make the clerks more comfortable letting you use them. Some town record offices that I visit on a fairly regular basis actually allow me to retrieve my own records from the vault, make my own copies, and so on. Having shown the staff, over many visits, that I am a professional who knows the proper way to handle important papers, I have been given certain privileges. This makes the visits more efficient for the clerk as well as for me. The clerk can take care of her day-to-day business without me disturbing her to get documents. I never abuse the privileges given to me. If I have any question as to whether I should or shouldn't copy a document, I will always defer to the clerk's opinion.

One very important point of etiquette is that you must leave all of the records and books in the same or better condition than you found them. Treating the books and documents as valuable tools for research will ensure that they are available for many years to come. Documents have actually been defaced or stolen by uncaring and greedy researchers over the years. Many probate records of famous people or sports stars have been stolen for the signature, which is then sold to collectors. Documents have also been taken by those who do not want to pay for copies, or who are just too lazy to make copies or transcriptions. Pages in old books have been cut out using razor blades and the like to save a few cents on photocopies or time. Since some books are too fragile to allow photocopying, you must allow yourself time to hand-transcribe the information. Stealing the pages or documents only makes it more difficult, or impossible, for another researcher to obtain the same information. Many restrictions have been placed on the use of old records due to this type of vandalism. Be conscious of these tactics and report any suspicious activity when you see it.

Important

You should also be exceptionally careful when using original documents. Some facilities will allow you to have more than one file or set of papers out at once. Make sure that you use only one set of papers at a time. Many researchers have inadvertently mixed up papers from several different files before they return the documents to the clerks. Once these papers are separated from the original file or packet, it is virtually impossible to find them again. One such occurrence resulted in my not being able to find an ancestor's probate record. I was excited to find an index citation for Joseph A. Rogers in the Rutland County, Vermont, probate index. The name and date were correct, so I went to the facility to look at the probate packet (the records had not been filmed). To my dismay, the packet was completely empty! Someone before me had either taken the papers or accidentally mixed them up in another file. I looked in all of the other Joseph Rogers probate packets, hoping that the researcher was searching all files bearing that name, to no avail. Until another researcher comes across the papers in another packet and brings them to the attention of the court clerk, these records may as well not exist. Since there is no microfilm copy to use as a backup, I may never see the probate package in question to determine if it was or wasn't the person I was researching.

When you are requesting information or documents from a facility by mail, there are some important things to consider. First of all, keep your request brief and to the point. Don't provide your entire family history in your letter. Make sure you specify what you need, provide all of the pertinent information to locate the record, and include payment if necessary. When writing to see if the facility has a particular record, it is also expedient to enclose a self-addressed stamped envelope for a reply. Make sure a handwritten letter is legible. If the recipient cannot read your writing, she isn't going to be able to provide you with any information. Include various spellings that you have encountered of the name in question. The staff member looking the name up may not be aware of the various spellings. Always be sure to include "please" and "thank you" in your letter. These magic words from our childhood still work wonders!

Tip

When I visit a church rectory or cemetery office that does not have a set fee schedule, I always make a small donation for the information I receive. The donation amount is based on the helpfulness of the clerk and the amount of information provided. There have been times when I have left a donation of ten to twenty dollars when the person has gone above and beyond the call of duty. I also thank the person who assists me and let them know how appreciative I am. Ask what the charge is and make an offer of a donation if they say "no charge." I always leave a donation, no matter how small. If they have looked for the information you requested and found nothing, a small donation is still in order. They did, after all, extend the effort to assist you.

When visiting small historical or genealogical societies, it is also a nice gesture to make a donation for services rendered. Remember that most of these organizations are run strictly by volunteers, and there are costs involved with keeping the information open and available for you to use. Making appropriate donations to aid the society will allow the group to provide services to others after you. Many of these organizations publish leaflets or books pertaining to the area or specialty. Purchasing one or more of these also helps support the organization.

One area of support that most people do not consider is giving volunteer time to a local repository or organization. If you use a facility on a regular basis, give back to the organization by giving of yourself. This can be done as part of a formal volunteer effort, or just by helping others that may be visiting while you are there. I have been at the local National Archives facility on many occasions when the staff and volunteers are very busy. When I see an individual waiting for a volunteer, or trying to figure out how to load the microfilm machine, I offer my assistance. The small amount of time and effort involved is a nice way of saying thanks to the volunteers that helped me when I was a "newbie" genealogist. We were all new at research at one time or another. Think back to the wonderful volunteers that guided you on your research journey, and then do the same for another researcher. The rewards are endless.

One such volunteer effort on my part actually led to my first paid job in the field of genealogy. I had recently donated a large manuscript to a local genealogical facility and was interested in the process that the manuscript would go through to become available to the general public. I asked the manuscript curator several questions regarding this process. In my discussion with him, it became apparent that the staff time was limited and it would take some time before my manuscript could be addressed. I was a bit disappointed at first, then offered to do the finding aid and cataloguing myself if the curator was willing to show me how. He was very enthusiastic about my offer, and I set out to learn how manuscripts were processed in this library.

Over the course of the next year (yes, it took that long since we only had a couple of hours each week to dedicate to it), a friend and I created the finding aid for the collection, catalogued it, and repacked all of the materials in acid-free folders and boxes to preserve it. During that time, I came to know the other library staff members and was offered a job as a part-time librarian. That first job blossomed into speaking engagements, a book contract, and a full-time position. I not only learned an incredible amount about manuscript processing, but also got the chance to see the other side of genealogical research. Working on both sides of the research process has made me aware of the positive and negative impact genealogical researchers have on societies and libraries as a whole. After working at a library desk, you know what approaches produce the best results and which approaches you never want to use.

Knowing as much as possible about the records you will be using, having a realistic expectation of what they will provide, and giving yourself ample time to use them will make your research more fruitful. When you are really pressed for time, you are more likely to miss important information contained in the documents. When we are stressed and have severe time constraints, we have a tendency to be more abrupt with those around us. This can result in even further time constraints. Being rude or demanding of the staff can actually slow down your productivity. Remind yourself that you are not the only demand on their time and there are others who need their assistance. Wait your turn, and ask politely. Always say "excuse me" if you must interrupt what they are doing. Be aware of others waiting behind you and do not monopolize the staff.

Some researchers seem to expect the staff to do the research for them. This attitude will cause frustration for both the staff and the researcher, since it is unrealistic to expect that anyone else will care as much about your family as you do. You are doing the research for your own satisfaction, and the staff is only there to assist you with access to the records and general research help. Yes, they probably know more about specific records than you do, but ask questions, learn as much as possible, and be grateful for the assistance they provide.

One example of a frustrating encounter occurred when I was working as a reference librarian in a large genealogical library. A patron approached me and asked,

Case Study

"Where do you keep the passenger lists from the 1700s?" My reply that there were no actual passenger lists from that time was not what she wanted to hear. She actually raised her voice loud enough for all to hear and stated, "There are indeed passenger lists from that time. Even the *Mayflower* had a passenger list. So, where are they?" I maintained my professional manner and explained that the *Mayflower* list was actually a compact, or contract, signed by some, but not necessarily all, of the passengers of the *Mayflower* vessel upon arrival on this continent. I further explained that passenger lists, as such, were not in general use until the mid-1800s and before that time, most were considered customs lists and were more likely to contain lists of goods transported than people. Obviously this was still not what she wanted to hear as she replied, "Fine. If you don't want to tell me where they are, then where are the naturalization records from the 1750s?" My reply was, "In England." Since the United States did not exist in the 1750s—it was a British colony—the records would have to be English in origin. She was rather abrupt in her departure, and I am sure she thought I was very unhelpful. If she had done her research into naturalization records and passenger lists (or U.S. history!) prior to coming to the library, she would have saved herself the trip. Remember that the staff can only provide items that actually exist!

Another such encounter was quite revealing. A college student approached the desk to ask about the availability of Polish records in our facility. I explained that we did not have any Polish records but that they might be available through the Family History Library in Salt Lake City. I suggested that she look at the library catalog to see if it listed any records of interest to her. Her reply was, "Oh, I already ordered those films, but those copies were all in Polish!" The researcher left, frustrated I'm sure, at not being able to access the records she wanted. Advance research into the holdings of the FHL and the microfilming project would have provided her with accurate information on what she might expect to find in the microfilmed records. Do your homework, and you will have much better results with far less time expended.

When you do as much research as possible before visiting the facility, you will have fewer frustrations and setbacks. The staff cannot "create" the documents you need, only provide you with assistance in finding and possibly interpreting them. Do not be afraid to ask for help or admit that you don't know something. There are no dumb questions. Trying to force a roll of microfilm onto a reader or printer because you don't know how it operates will only damage the equipment and your pride when you have to tell the staff that it is broken. Many of the new copiers and readers are complex pieces of machinery and require the utmost care. Careless users can damage machines and it may take several days or weeks to repair. During that time, other researchers cannot access the records either, so please be careful and respectful of the expensive equipment. Take a moment to review the procedures and machines as well as information about the records and the facility. This is especially important if it is your first visit or if it has been a while since

Timesaver

you were there. If you were unable to get advance information about the holdings and access rules, taking a moment to do so will save you many trips to the reference desk to ask questions.

Having a can-do attitude is also a real plus. The staff at the library I worked in had a saying we used when we encountered a pessimistic researcher: "We don't let people give up here." Most often the phrase was the result of a patron's hesitation to use some of the technical machines, such as automatic microfilm readers or printers. To the researcher who comes whining back to the desk saying, "I can't find the roll of microfilm," our response might be, "If you can't find the roll, how do you expect to find your ancestor?" These comments, offered in a lighthearted manner, go a long way toward putting people at ease. Don't take yourself too seriously or be so intense in your research that you don't enjoy the trip. Keep in mind that we are all researching because we enjoy it. The rewards far outweigh the obstacles. The harder you work to find that stubborn ancestor, the more pleasure you will get when you finally pin him down!

All in all, if you approach the research facilities and staff in a positive, upbeat attitude, the same will usually be returned to you. Rudeness breeds rudeness, and courtesy promotes courtesy. Put yourself in the other person's shoes and then act accordingly. Be polite to fellow researchers and staff, keep conversations low and to a minimum, treat the documents as the precious items they are, and you will enjoy the rewards you will reap!

TEN

Some Final Thoughts

Warning

G enealogical research is a rewarding experience. You will learn amazing facts about your ancestors, geography, and history, but most of all, you will learn about yourself.

Genealogical research is one hobby that requires using original records, microfilm, the Internet, and all of the other tools that are available. **There is no database in a computer somewhere that has your family's ancestry all done, in spite of what many people think.** Even if there were such a database, I am not sure I would use it. Over the years I have come to appreciate the search as much as the results. There is something so satisfying about looking down at a record that includes a picture or signature of one of your ancestors. Touching the same pages they touched, walking the same streets they walked, and learning as much about them as possible will help you put your own life in perspective. I have learned that times were not better then or now, only different. There are many things that we have in common with our ancestors as they helped make us who we are through their perseverance, tenacity, and just plain courage to overcome the obstacles presented to them. There is no easy way to fill in those pedigree and family group sheets, but investing your time and energy to do it pays its own rewards.

Regardless of whether you are twenty or sixty-five years old, working full time or retired, you can continue to research your family history. Over the ten plus years that I have been compiling my pedigree charts and family groups sheets, I have survived two teenage daughters, a husband who was routinely on his way to the airport for another business trip, held a grueling sixty-hour a week job in the retail sector, volunteered at a library, and maintained my home. Balancing all of the tasks and obligations required of us is actually easier when you manage to include doing things you enjoy. Genealogical research is my outlet, my passion, and even my addiction. Utilizing my time in the most efficient manner has resulted in streamlining all other aspects of my life. Organization just feels good, saves time, and eliminates some (but not all) frustration.

Implementing the suggestions and tips presented in this book will save you time, make your research more efficient and productive, and give you a sense of pride in your work that will carry over into your nongenealogical life. I realized, after organizing my research and files, that I was using some of the ideas to organize my home and my life. I have become a list maker and never venture out of the house to do errands without at least two or three items on my "to do" list. It has become a challenge to get as many tasks done in one trip as possible. I just love to cross things off the list as they are completed, don't you? Approach your research and daily routines with the same determination and preparation, and you will discover just how much can be accomplished. Enjoy *every* minute of the wonderful journey.

Forms for Genealogists

Following are blank copies of forms referred to throughout *The Weekend Genealogist*:

- Vital Records Log Sheet (page 123)
- Vital Records Form for Foreign Country Research (page 124)
- Soundex Cards (page 125)
- Census Overview Form (page 126)
- Correspondence Log (page 127)
- Surname Overview Form (page 128)
- City Directory Log Sheet (page 129)

You are free to photocopy them for your personal use. No use in printed work is permitted without permission.

NAME	TOWN	YEAR	VOL	PAGE	CKED

Vital Records Log Sheet
You are free to copy this form for personal use. For discussion of it, see page 13.

Town/Village _____ Region _____ Country _____

YEAR	TYPE	CERT #	NAME	COPIED	SEARCHED	TRANSC.	DONE

Vital Records Form for Foreign Country Research
You are free to copy this form for personal use. For discussion of it, see page 14.

Census _____ Soundex Code _____ State _____
Vol. _____ E.D. _____
Head of Family _____ Sheet _____ Line _____
color _____ month _____ year _____ age _____ birthplace _____ citizenship _____
County _____
City _____ Street _____ House# _____

	Name	Rel	Mo	Yr	Age	Birthplace	Citizen
1							
2							
3							
4							
5							
6							
7							
8							

Census _____ Soundex Code _____ State _____
Vol. _____ E.D. _____
Head of Family _____ Sheet _____ Line _____
color _____ month _____ year _____ age _____ birthplace _____ citizenship _____
County _____
City _____ Street _____ House# _____

	Name	Rel	Mo	Yr	Age	Birthplace	Citizen
1							
2							
3							
4							
5							
6							
7							
8							

Census _____ Soundex Code _____ State _____
Vol. _____ E.D. _____
Head of Family _____ Sheet _____ Line _____
color _____ month _____ year _____ age _____ birthplace _____ citizenship _____
County _____
City _____ Street _____ House# _____

	Name	Rel	Mo	Yr	Age	Birthplace	Citizen
1							
2							
3							
4							
5							
6							
7							
8							

Census _____ Soundex Code _____ State _____
Vol. _____ E.D. _____
Head of Family _____ Sheet _____ Line _____
color _____ month _____ year _____ age _____ birthplace _____ citizenship _____
County _____
City _____ Street _____ House# _____

	Name	Rel	Mo	Yr	Age	Birthplace	Citizen
1							
2							
3							
4							
5							
6							
7							
8							

Soundex Cards

You are free to copy this form for personal use. For discussion of it, see page 15.

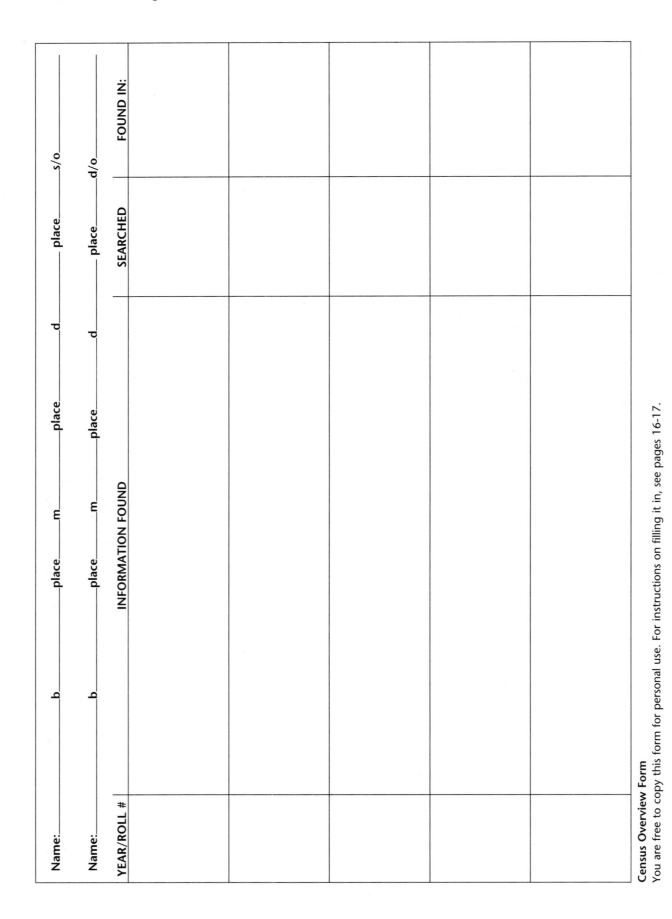

Name: _____ b _____ place _____ m _____ place _____ d _____ place _____ s/o _____			
Name: _____ b _____ place _____ m _____ place _____ d _____ place _____ d/o _____			
YEAR/ROLL #	INFORMATION FOUND	SEARCHED	FOUND IN:

Census Overview Form
You are free to copy this form for personal use. For instructions on filling it in, see pages 16-17.

DATE	NAME/ADDRESS	REASON FOR LETTER	RESPONSE

Correspondence Log
You are free to copy this form for personal use. For discussion of it, see page 19.

NAME							

NOTES

Surname Overview Form
You are free to copy this form for personal use. For instructions for filling it in, see page 20.

NAME	YEAR	CITY	SPOUSE	OCCUP.	WORK ADDRESS/HOME ADDRESS

City Directory Log Sheet
You are free to copy this form for personal use. For discussion of it, see page 93.

Bibliography

Arends, Marthe. *Genealogy on CD-ROM*. Baltimore: Genealogical Publishing Co., 1999.

———. *Genealogy Software Guide*. Baltimore: Genealogical Publishing Co., 1998.

Bentley, Elizabeth Petty. *The Genealogist's Address Book*, 4th ed. Baltimore: Genealogical Publishing Co., 1998.

———. *County Courthouse Book*, 2nd ed. Baltimore: Genealogical Publishing Co., 1995.

Carmack, Sharon DeBartolo. *The Genealogy Sourcebook*. Los Angeles: Lowell House, 1997.

———. *Organizing Your Family History Search*. Cincinnati, Betterway Books, 1999.

Croom, Emily Anne. *The Unpuzzling Your Past Workbook: Essential Forms and Letters for All Genealogists*. Cincinnati: Betterway Books, 1996.

———. *The Genealogist's Companion and Sourcebook: A Beyond-the-Basics, Hands-On Guide to Unpuzzling Your Past*. Cincinnati: Betterway Books, 1994.

Crowe, Elizabeth Powell. *Genealogy Online*, Millennium ed. New York: McGraw-Hill, 2000.

Dollarhide, William and William Thorndale. *Map Guide to the U.S. Federal Censuses 1790-1920*. Baltimore: Genealogical Publishing Co., 1987.

Dollarhide, William. *The Census Book: A Genealogist's Guide to Federal Census Facts, Schedules, and Indexes*. Bountiful, Utah: Heritage Quest, 1999.

Drake, Paul. *What Did They Mean By That? A Dictionary of Historical Terms for Genealogists*. Bowie, Md.: Heritage Books, 1994.

———. *What Did They Mean By That? Some More Words, Volume 2*. Bowie, Md.: Heritage Books, 1998.

Eichholz, Alice, ed. *Ancestry's Red Book: American State, County & Town Sources*. Rev. ed. Salt Lake City: Ancestry, Inc., 1992.

Evans, Barbara Jean. *A to Zax: A Comprehensive Genealogical Dictionary for Genealogists and Historians*. Alexandria, Va.: Hearthside Press, 1995.

Guide to Genealogical Research in the National Archives. Washington, DC: National Archives Trust Fund Board, 1985.

Everton, George. *The Handy Book for Genealogists—United States of America*. 9th ed. Logan, Utah: Everton Publishers, 1998.

Helm, Matthew L. and April Leigh Helm. *Genealogy Online for Dummies*. Foster City, Calif.: IDG Books Worldwide, 1998.

Howells, Cyndi. *Netting Your Ancestors: Genealogical Research on the Internet*. Baltimore: Genealogical Publishing Co., 1997.

Kemp, Thomas Jay. *International Vital Records Handbook,* 3rd ed. Baltimore: Genealogical Publishing Co., 1995.

Lackey, Richard. *Cite Your Sources.* Jackson: University Press of Mississippi, 1985.

Levine, John, Margaret Levine Young and Carol Baroudi. *The Internet for Dummies,* 4th ed. Foster City, Calif.: IDG Books Worldwide, 1999.

Mills, Elizabeth Shown. *Evidence! Citation and Analysis for the Family Historian.* Baltimore: Genealogical Publishing Co., 1997.

Morgan, George G. *The Genealogy Forum on America Online: The Official User's Guide.* Salt Lake City: Ancestry, Inc. 1998.

Rose, Christine and Kay Germain Ingalls. *The Complete Idiot's Guide to Genealogy.* New York: Alpha Books, 1997.

Saldana, Richard, ed. *A Practical Guide to the "Misteaks" Made in Census Indexes.* Bountiful, Utah: American Genealogical Lending Library, 1987.

Smith, Juliana Szucs. *The Ancestry Family Historian's Address Book.* Salt Lake City: Ancestry, Inc., 1997.

Sperry, Kip. *Reading Early American Handwriting.* Baltimore: Genealogical Publishing Co., 1998.

Szucs, Loretto Dennis and Sandra Hargreaves Luebking, eds. *The Source: A Guidebook of America Genealogy,* Rev. ed. Salt Lake City: Ancestry, Inc., 1997.

200 Years of U.S. Census Taking: Population and Housing Questions, 1790-1990. Washington, DC: U.S. Department of Commerce, Bureau of the Census, 1992.

Warren, James W. and Paula Stuart Warren. *Getting the Most Mileage From Genealogical Research Trips,* 3rd ed. St. Paul, Minn.: Warren Research and Marketing, 1998.

Index